The Mystery of the Incarnation

The
Mystery
of
the Incarnation

Cardinal Basil Hume OSB

DARTON · LONGMAN + TODD

First published in 1999 by
Darton, Longman and Todd Ltd
1 Spencer Court
140–142 Wandsworth High Street
London SW18 4JJ

Reprinted 2000

ISBN 0–232–52354–1

A catalogue record for this book is available from the British Library

Designed and produced by Sandie Boccacci
using QuarkXPress on an Apple PowerMac 7500
Set in 12/15pt Berling
Printed and bound in Great Britain
by The Cromwell Press, Trowbridge, Wiltshire

Mystery

The meaning of things, and their purpose,
Is in part now hidden
But shall in the end become clear.
The choice is between
The Mystery and the absurd.
To embrace the Mystery
Is to discover the real.
It is to walk towards the light,
To glimpse the morning star,
To catch sight from time to time
Of what is truly real.
It is no more than a flicker of light
Through the cloud of unknowing,
A fitful ray of light
That is a messenger from the sun
Which is hidden from your gaze.
You see the light but not the sun.
When you set yourself to look more closely,
You will begin to see some sense
In the darkness that surrounds you.
Your eyes will begin to pick out
The shape of things and persons around you.
You will begin to see in them
The presence of the One
Who gives them meaning and purpose,
And that it is He
Who is the explanation of them all.

Cardinal Basil Hume OSB

Contents

❧

Celebrating the Incarnation

Preface

In late 1998 Cardinal Hume published *The Mystery of the Cross*, a collection of meditations on suffering and death. As soon as it was finished he began work on a companion volume, to be called *The Mystery of the Incarnation*. He saw these books as an invitation to meditate on the need for Jesus Christ in our own lives and in the life of society. He was particularly concerned that Christ might be sidelined in the millennium celebrations, and wanted to focus attention on the fundamental Christian mystery – of God becoming man 2000 years ago.

He asked me to help him with editing the homilies and talks from which this book has been compiled. He approved the final proofs just before he went into hospital in May, and from there he hoped to add a short introduction. He told me that he had a theme running through his mind, based on the last words Jesus spoke from the cross. In the event his advancing illness prevented him from writing it. But it so happens that only weeks before – on Good Friday – he had given a broadcast on BBC Radio 4 on exactly this theme, the Seven Last Words of Jesus. Accordingly, and with the kind permission of the BBC, we have reproduced this as an introduction to the book.

HEATHER CRAUFURD
July 1999

Introduction

A loved one is dying. It is natural to crowd around the bed to catch a sentence or a word that those parched lips may utter. Such words are precious for they are the last testament of the loved one, and a message to be treasured.

What exactly did Jesus say, what was his meaning? Those Last Words are to be pondered, discussed, explored. He spoke Seven Words. They were heard by his mother Mary as she stood at the foot of the cross, by his beloved disciple John, by Mary of Magdala and others. They were messages for them, but not for them only. His words are for all time, addressed to every person, thus to you and to me. We join Mary and those others who stood at the foot of the cross, and we listen prayerfully.

'Father, forgive them, for they know not what they do.' Jesus prayed thus as they drove the nails into his hands and feet. Is there one of us who can claim to be in no need of forgiveness? Not I, at any rate. But do not be distressed, much less despairing. He wants to forgive, even, dare I say it, to find an excuse for our wrongdoing: *'they know not what they do.'* I have but to recognise my need for forgiveness, be sorry for the way I have offended, and resolve to do my best from now on and he forgives. He wants to. Lovers do.

There is of course more, much more. Jesus wants our companionship. He came among us, God made man, to draw us to friendship with him and for all time. God made us for himself. God is the most lovable of all that is lovable. He is the most beautiful of all that is beautiful. We are destined to experience that love and that beauty. We are made to be with God and to enjoy for all time the moment of ecstatic joy such as lovers know. But, Lord, I am not worthy. You are perfect, I am not. I am selfish, arrogant and my life is far from being blameless.

'This day you will be with me in paradise.' 'Lord, remember me when you come into your kingdom.' That good thief spoke for us all. From his cross and his agony, he was our teacher and is so today: 'Remember me.'

'This day you will be with me in paradise.' When will that be for you and me? We do not know. But if we pray with sorrow and sincerity in our hearts, 'Remember me', he will not forget us. He cannot for he does not want to. That explains another Word which he spoke from the Cross:

'I thirst.' We are told that crucifixion induces a terrible thirst. The dying man longs for a drink. '*I thirst*', he said. John the beloved disciple records that Word. But John was a thoughtful writer, not just a recorder of events. He understood a deeper meaning in that word '*I thirst*'. When Jesus spoke it he was expressing his longing for those whom he loved, his longing therefore for all of us. He longs for us to allow him to be part of our lives, to admit him into our thinking and into our hearts. He knocks at the door of our lives. It is for us to invite him

to enter or not. He does not force his way in. He wants us to be free. '*I thirst*', he said. They did not give him water, they gave him vinegar to drink for it is supposed to act like a drug. But vinegar is sour, uncongenial to drink. It is bitter. Is the response of many of us to his thirsting no more than a sour, or even bitter, response?

'*Woman, behold your son.*' What did his mother feel at that moment? She would have quenched his thirst with water, fresh and life-giving, as she had done so often in the past. But she could do no more than go on standing, a sword piercing her heart again and again. A mother would be by the side of her suffering son or daughter. It is part of her role as mother. So she will be at your side and mine now, and especially when we come to die. She is our mother too. '*Woman, behold your son*', he said to her as his gaze went to John, to whom he said: '*Son, behold your mother.*' Those pains of hers were new birth pangs. We were being born into God's family through the death he was enduring and his rising again from the dead. She was now Mother again, Mother of those to be born in the waters of Baptism.

'*My God, my God, why hast Thou forsaken me?*' Meanwhile the end for Jesus was drawing ever nearer. His death was no easy one. The excruciating physical pain is hard to imagine. But there is clearly more. He was praying the opening words of the psalm: '*My God, my God, why hast thou forsaken me?*' What darkness of mind was he experiencing? To feel abandoned by a loved one is a great pain. But the sense that God no longer cares, or is leaving us to the mercy of the foes that can so easily invade our minds and hearts, that is the greater agony. A voice, mocking and cynical, calls within us: 'There is no God, there is nothing after death, only nothing, you have lived in vain.' Did he want to undergo that experience of depression, mental agony, the sense of being abandoned, for our sake? I believe that he did. When afflicted with an inner agony of mind and heart, it is good to remember that this was the experience of Jesus too, both on the cross and in the Garden of Gethsemane. Mental suffering and desolation have been sanctified and given meaning because Jesus knew both of them.

'Into thy hands, Lord, I commend my spirit.' Then he prayed aloud again. The verse of another psalm provided him with the words: *'Into thy hands, Lord, I commend my spirit.'* At the moment when he was experiencing abandonment by God his Father, he spoke words denoting his abandoning of himself into the hands of God. It is a remarkable expression of trust and love to entrust oneself to another at the time when all the reasons for doing so appear to be absent. Do you sense an absence of God in your life? Pain, misfortune, bewilderment may at this moment, or at some other time, be your companions. You cannot see any way of escaping from the feeling of being trapped. It is heroic to pray: 'Into your hands, Lord, I commend my spirit.' That prayer brings peace. It does not remove the pain, or not normally so, but deep down within we have found words to make us one with Christ in his agony. We join him in his self-giving to his Father. We are at one with him in his sacrifice for he died in order to overcome sin and death.

Why it had to be thus I, for my part, do not know. Could not God have found some other means to rid the world of sin and its wages of death? I would have to be God himself to know how to answer that question. I am content to wait until I see God in vision to be able to see how his purposes have been at work in our best interests. But this I do know: God in becoming man shared the human condition. He would be one of us, make holy our human experiences, good and bad, save of course for sin; give them meaning and significance and then enable them to lead us to the new life, life hidden with Christ in God.

'It is finished.' Now the end has come. 'It is finished', he said, and he bowed his head and gave up his spirit. Death creates an emptiness in the hearts of those who loved the one who has died. Mary of Magdala, sorrowing and seeking to be consoled, came to the tomb early while it was still dark and there, remarkably, saw that the stone had been taken away from the tomb. The end was a new beginning. Hearts would rejoice again, darkness give way to light. Christ had risen from the dead.

The Mystery
of the Incarnation

The meaning of things, and their purpose,
Is in part now hidden
But shall in the end become clear.
The choice is between
The Mystery and the absurd.

'All their eyes were fixed on him'

T he more I have reflected on those words in St Luke's Gospel – 'All eyes in the synagogue were fixed on him' (Luke 4:20) – the more they have suggested to me what should be the theme of the days leading up to the celebration of the millennium, the Holy Year.

All eyes were fixed on him. That is for us. All our eyes should be fixed on him, and if they are not then our celebration of the millennium will be an empty celebration, because the whole point of celebrating the year 2000 is to remember that Jesus became man – God became man. That is the good news by which we must live and which, by our example, we have to share with other people. The very centre of our lives has to be Jesus Christ, true God and true man.

On one occasion, when Jesus was speaking to his close followers, the apostle Philip said to Our Lord: 'Just show us the Father, let us see God and we shall be satisfied.' Our Lord answered him: 'Have I been with you all this time, and you do not understand that to see me is to see the Father?' We cannot see God in our present state. He lies quite beyond our capacity to understand him, see him or touch him. But because he became man, through studying his words and watching his actions, then we get some idea of what God is like. To see him is to see the Father.

On another occasion the apostle Thomas asked Our Lord: 'Lord we do not know where you are going so how can we know the way?' (John 4:5) and he answered: 'I am the way, the truth and the life.' If we want the truth about who we are, what we are destined for, it is Jesus Christ who teaches us. If we want to know the way to travel through this world and have a future in the next, he is the way. If we want to be filled with his life, it is from him that we receive it.

That opens up for us what we are all destined for, or indeed made for, which is after death to enjoy the vision of God face to face. That experience will be the total fulfilment of all that we have desired in this life, all the best for which we aimed.

It is sad that there are so many people who simply do not know what lies before them after death: a moment of ecstatic love which will never cease and of which we can never be deprived. That is a wonderful thought and one which consoles us so much when we have lost a close relative, lost a dear friend, lost a colleague, as so many of us have experienced.

The Great Jubilee of the Year 2000

A Year of Opportunity

❧

We are now walking together into the next millennium. Once we are into the year 2000 the Millennium Candle will have been extinguished, the resolution a distant echo and there will be the danger that for many people life will carry on as usual. But it must not be so. It is important that we make the most of what will be a year of opportunity, when we can underline our commitment as Christians, individually and collectively, to the well-being of our planet and its people.

If we do not put Christ at the centre of the celebration of the millennium then we risk making that celebration no more than a commercial extravaganza or a celebration of human achievement. That kind of celebration has its place no doubt. But it is not enough. It is the birth of Christ that we shall be celebrating. The crib will always be more important than the dome. As Christians we must be proud of our faith and profess it. At the same time we want, of course, to walk with those of other faiths and religions, we respecting them and they respecting us. They will respect us the more if we are true to ourselves.

Let us start now to prepare for Christmas Day 1999. It is the day when the celebration of the millennium should begin. We must make this Christmas Day truly special. Do not let commercial considerations prevail. Do not permit others to empty Christmas of its religious significance. Do not allow claims that we are no longer a Christian nation to become an accepted orthodoxy. Do not listen to cynical non-believers who deride our Christian efforts. The time has come for us to proclaim and celebrate the riches of our different churches. The time has come to cease carping about the limitations and faults of our different churches. Of course we are not perfect. We have never claimed to be so. But we must now move forward with a renewed enthusiasm to preach the Gospel and especially to those who have never heard it.

There has been much planning to prepare for the millennium and its celebration. This of course is right and proper, and we are indebted to those who have been engaged in this work. But I suggest that as we reflect together we should concentrate not so much on what sort of world we want to create in the new millennium, but rather on what kind of people we should become. We will not, and cannot, change the world unless and until we change ourselves.

In Rome on Christmas Eve, the Pope will open the great bronze door to mark the opening of the Christian millennium, the beginning of the Holy Year, a gesture which has taken place every 25 years since the year 1425. We might remember that there is a door at which the Pilgrim who comes to us from afar has been knocking, your door and mine. He wants to gain access into our minds and, most important, into our hearts. We admit him or keep him out. It is our choice (Revelation 3:20–22).

But surely our celebration of the year 2000 can only be measured in terms of that journey of conversion that each one of us is called to make, for the call to conversion is the indispensable condition of Christian love. The Lord's command, 'Repent and believe the Gospel' should ring in our ears as we take every step on our pilgrimage into the millennium and beyond. We should all aim to cross the threshold of the third millennium different, better people.

As Christians we are commanded by Christ to witness to the Gospel. In our society today there are many people searching. They are in search of happiness, of a peace which the world cannot bring. They seek authentic values, standards and, above all, reasons for living and hoping. Have we anything to say to them? Of course we have. It is incumbent on each of us as individuals and Christian communities to lay aside our divisions – lay aside, I say: not pretend they do not exist – in order to speak to the nation of the things of God and his Gospel, to describe our pilgrimage of faith, and to show them that it leads to life hidden with Christ in God, which is the fulfilment of every human aspiration.

Our responsibility is to live lives that witness to the truth about God, who in Christ saved the world. At the dawn of a new millennium we are there to tell the world that the ultimate and universal source of all hope in the future is to be found in him, and him alone. Christ must be born again into our society in the year 2000. Yes, it must be so.

What Does Christmas Mean to You?

❦

I was once at a peace rally in Trafalgar Square and was one of those who had a place on the platform. It was just before Christmas. After the rally we had to make our way through a large crowd. As we did so, media reporters tried to get comments from us. One, to my astonishment, said to me: 'What does Christmas mean to you?' I was rather taken aback because it didn't seem to me to be immediately relevant to the purpose of the rally. I had to react at once and said the first thing that came into my head. It was this: 'The great and awesome God became man for me.' He said 'thank you' and didn't pursue the subject. It was only after I had gone fifteen yards or so that it dawned on me what I had said. Here was a familiar truth which I had known all my life. But at that moment the simple truth that God had become man seemed to me quite staggering, and I realised I was looking at a familiar truth in a new way.

It is so easy to celebrate Christmas and miss the main point, or become so familiar with the Christian teaching about it that it fails to make its impact. It should have a profound effect upon our lives. It is a feast at which we celebrate God's entry into our world as man. He entered into our world in order to enter into our lives. He came to share what we are, to give meaning to what we do, to heal wounds, to give life. Am I prepared to let him into my life? Or, to put the question another way, do I see him as a possible intruder to be excluded, or as a guest to be welcomed?

St John says 'God is love', not that he loves but that he is entirely love. That is why I have come to treasure each Christmas. I have come to realise more intensely that the birth of Jesus Christ in that stable in Bethlehem is where all my questions begin to be answered. If I want to look on the face of utter love, if I want to see what the lover will do for the beloved, I have to take myself with faith to the crib and look at the image of the child lying in the manger. The celebration of Christmas is empty and futile without the enduring belief that this child is indeed the Christ, son of the living God. God has entered, still enters, our world. He comes as gently as an infant child; he will share all our growing, our living, our loving, our grieving and dying.

In St Paul's Cathedral there hangs a picture painted in 1904 by William Holman Hunt called *The Light of the World*. In that picture, Jesus Christ is seen standing at a closed door. In one hand he carries a lamp and with the other he is knocking at the door. On the outside there is neither knob nor handle. The visitor can only enter if the person within opens the door from the inside. Jesus Christ does not force himself on us. That is why there is no handle on the outside of the door in the picture.

But Jesus Christ is knocking all the time at your door and mine. Are we entirely free to say 'Yes, come in'? Or do we refuse to react to that persistent knock? We have to have faith and confidence to open the door to let him into our lives. And when we open the door we see that he is carrying the lamp. He will be the light, a kindly light to guide us:

> Lead, kindly light, amid the encircling gloom.
> Lead Thou me on. . . . Keep Thou my feet,
> I do not ask to see the distant scene,
> One step enough for me.

We do not see the distant scene. The future is hidden from us and we have to be content to take one step at a time. How important it is to go forward with confidence. That reporter, I now see, had asked the really important question at the peace rally: 'What does Christmas mean to you?' Let him into your life. Let him take you wherever he may lead you. He knows the way and he carries the lamp. Indeed he *is* the Way, the Truth and the Life.

A Christmas Meditation

❦

Oxford Street was crowded, very crowded. It was late afternoon, mid-week in November. Trade was brisk, or appeared to be so, even though Christmas was still far off. The people seemed very pre-occupied as they darted in and out of the shops. Their hands, baskets, plastic bags laden with gifts.

Later, in a very different part of the world families were making their way despondently along a dry and dusty road. They were looking for food. They had left their homes and with them carried – well, they had nothing to carry save their hungry children, strapped to their backs.

Then I saw the tinsel, the lights and the beautifully arranged goods in the shop windows; children looking in with wonder in their eyes, alive with expectation. Then a little later, I looked into the crying eyes of a starving child and saw their sadness, perhaps even terror, and a dullness that comes when hope has gone.

To the north nearly two thousand years ago a man and his wife trod the dusty roads of Palestine. It was the road to Bethlehem. They had to register. The edict of

Caesar Augustus had decreed it. They had travelled far, so there was no place left where they could rest in comfort. The inn was full, there was no room.

Her time had come. She gave birth in a stable, in poverty, unknown, unwanted even. It was the burst of song from they knew not where that told some shepherds of this birth. The voices sang: 'Glory to God in the highest, and peace to men of goodwill.' The shepherds were in awe, wondering at the meaning of it all, and so they went to Bethlehem. They sensed that something strange had taken place.

The child was small and weak, no different from other newly born babies, but there was something else – something which at first was beyond their understanding. They sensed it but could not explain. But they had that power which good and simple people often have, which is to see things as they are without allowing learning and worldly values to cloud their judgement. It is a child's gift to be direct and not be surprised by truths that lie beyond their grasp. They saw a child lying in a manger, no more than that, but they slowly understood what was hidden.

Several thousand miles away the shoppers continued to rush here and there, to make ready the preparations which were still several weeks away. There were presents to buy, turkeys to purchase and many other tasks to be performed. There was no time to think, no space to pause and find the reason for this great feasting.

Life's journey is over rough and dusty roads, and we can often be wearied by it and weak from lack of food.

I mean that aching pain of a life without meaning or purpose, of fear of an unknown future and of death itself. It is a life without hope, lived often in the midst of plenty, with riches and goods that do not nourish the spirit.

Spiritual hunger has its pains too, but they are healing pains when we hunger for what is true, for what is good, for what is beautiful, for love itself in its purest form. That is when we hunger for God. I must often wait for him to feed me. I must wait, not rushing around hectically, not over concerned with the riches of this world. Not by bread alone does man live, but by every word that comes from God. That word speaks of things that no eye has seen, and that have never entered into the mind. It is of the mystery of love that the word speaks, food for our starving souls, and it is he, the bread of life, come to take away our spiritual hunger.

So he lies there in the stable, poor, weak and unnoticed by many. But the angels continue to sing 'Glory to God in the highest' for they see the glory of the Lord in that small child. The children get out the tinsel, make the tree look good, rejoice and rightly so, for it is Christmas. They will waken on that day with wonder in their eyes, alive with expectation, for their eyes will glimpse for a moment the glory of the Lord hidden from the worldly, but shown to those who become as little children.

And many thousands of miles away where the roads are dry and dusty, thousands of little children will be happy because those who shopped in Oxford Street have not forgotten them. They have given to the starving their concern, their prayers and their help. And those for whom there are no worldly goods, he will surely enrich with the warmth and intimacy of his love. To those, too, generous givers of concern and help, he will give as well, gifts beyond all price, the knowledge and love of him.

We have seen a child, lying in a manger, that is all, but we have understood what was hidden from the eye: God who became man.

God So Loved the World

※

> God so loved the world that he gave his only Son, that whoever believes in him should not perish but have eternal life. (John 3:16)

There was no room for them in the inn. The world went on in its own way, event following on event, uninterested and unconcerned about the great event that would take place, not in the inn but in a cave. The people at that time were hardly to be blamed, for after all they did not know what was taking place in Bethlehem. Is it the same for us? The event has taken place, the most important event in the whole of history: God became man. Our generation cannot be excused for being uninterested and unconcerned.

The world may be uninterested and unconcerned, but God is not. He is most interested and most concerned. Otherwise how could it have been said 'God so loved the world that he gave his only Son'? He so loved the world – that is the key to understanding the Incarnation. God so loved the world – that does not mean a vague and rather general feeling of goodwill for what we call 'the world'. No, that love of God which prompted the coming of God the Son to become one of us is a personal love for each one of us. The sending of his Son is to each of us personally and individually. God never looks at crowds, he sees only the individual. That is the Christmas gift which is the reason for the presents we give each other; a reminder of the greatest of all gifts: God's love to each one of us.

He wants to enter into our lives, and desperately so, not into our lives in general but into each person's life. Is there room in your heart for him? Can he find space in your thinking? Can he find a place in your loving? Or is there no room because you have other interests, other ambitions, other preoccupations, and so he inevitably is crowded out? If he is crowded out of your life he cannot give you his most precious gift – life, life with him forever.

Perhaps you feel your heart and mind are not ready for him, but do not let that be the reason for not letting him into your life, because when he brings his love he brings forgiveness if we are truly sorry and anxious to change. He wants to find space in your mind and heart, but you must make sure that space is available.

Never forget the deepest meaning of the Incarnation: that God so loved the world, so loved you, that he came to find space in your mind and in your heart where he can be with you and you with him.

Seeking the Transcendent

❦

How can we begin to grow and see in the events of life the hand of God, and see in each other the face of Christ? St Paul suggests the answer:

> Let your thoughts be on heavenly things, not on the things that are in the earth. (Col. 3:2)

That is the secret. Look beyond and above the things of men and earth. It is there – paradoxically, surprisingly and unexpectedly – that we begin to see the hand of God in the events of daily life, the face of Christ dimly outlined among those whom we know and love.

We have to seek constantly the transcendent, plunge more deeply into the mystery that is God, and worship him more reverently. Like him we must establish and deepen community life. We must refuse to be intimidated by opposition or oppression. We must seek every means of communicating freely with the peoples of today who, no matter under what political system they live, are starved of the word of truth and of the bread of life.

Christic, both God and Man

᪥

> ... For us men and for our salvation, he came
> down from heaven; by the power of the Holy
> Spirit he became incarnate from the Virgin Mary,
> and was made man ...

Those words from the Creed do not, perhaps,
immediately inspire our minds or warm our
hearts. But they should do so. They are important, and familiar as well, for they are part of our
prayer on every feast day and at our Sunday worship.
They are words written over sixteen hundred years ago,
carefully chosen after much debate, and often following bitter controversy.

They are words never quite equal to expressing the
secrets about God which they are trying to convey;
words that nevertheless proclaim, and in solemn
manner, that Christ – that babe in the manger – is both
God and man.

Now those words of the Creed are a summary of the
truth about Christ which are to be accepted by believers, a test of orthodoxy, necessary for Baptism. They

are to be sung or said with voice and heart in accord. They are truths that give hope to those in search of meaning and purpose, truths hidden from the wise and clever, but revealed to those still young in mind and open to new discoveries and fresh surprises.

> We believe in one Lord Jesus Christ, the only Son of God ... God from God, Light from Light, true God from true God ...

These words are but a formula – abstract, cold and unreal – unless our minds and hearts are touched; that is, unless our hearts are involved in our prayer and our prayer involves our hearts.

It is only gradually that the words of Scripture and of the Creed reveal something of their inner meaning. It is like the viewing of a landscape. The more we look the more we see. The eye cannot, at first glance, convey to the mind all the beauty that lies before it, nor study every detail that is part of the whole. It needs time, patience, persistence before the eye becomes one with the reality it is contemplating, and it with the eye.

The act of faith is a groping of the mind to accept as true what God has revealed and has been handed down to us and taught by the Church both yesterday and today. Sometimes in confident mood we pray: 'Lord, I do believe.' At other times when doubt threatens to take control we must add: 'Lord, help thou my unbelief.'

There is more merit in a step taken in the dark than one that costs no effort or pain when the way is clear. That can lead to the surrender of our minds to the truth we could not, unaided, discover for ourselves, and even when accepted cannot ever fully understand. This is the truth that he is both God and man, and this we must affirm; that is the beginning of a new journey into the mystery of God, a voyage of discovery as we go in search of truth. Remember it is the refusal to believe that hurts him, not the struggle to do so. Faith is the surrendering of our minds, but it is also the surrendering of our hearts. It is perhaps more natural to follow the promptings of our hearts. Faith is an encounter with a person. It is love meeting love. He meets us first so as to give direction to the waywardness of our affections. He struggles to find space within our crowded hearts, but too often we tell him there is no room. The words of the Creed do not achieve their real purpose unless they lead us to the person about whom we say: 'We believe in Jesus Christ ... true God from true God.'

Human and Divine Meet
in Christ

❧

In all our emptiness and failure we can and must turn always to the fulfilment of God's covenant with humanity. The Word became flesh and dwelt amongst us. It is in Christ that the human and divine meet. God emptied himself and became as we are in all except our sinfulness. Through the Incarnation, God's taking of our human nature and his involvement in our human history has redeemed all that is human and given it a glory that no subsequent sin and rebellion can ever ultimately deface or destroy. Our human world, our humanity, is refashioned in Christ and is assured of an everlasting destiny.

To come to him in faith, to die with him in order to live to God, opens up for us a new creation, new heavens and a new earth, in which we see God in Christ and discern the face of God.

'Have I been with you so long,' said Jesus, 'and you do not know me, Philip? He who has seen me has seen the Father; so how can you say "Show us the

Father"? Do you not believe that I am in the Father and the Father is in me?' (John 14:9–10)

To imagine that we still cannot 'put a face' to God, that we are still in the dark about the reality of divine love and compassion, is to ignore perhaps the blindingly obvious, and fail to linger long enough on the features and the personality of Jesus Christ.

Here surely we can learn to enter into 'conversation' with God. The words of Our Lord and his every action are recorded in time but are 'outside' time, as relevant and grace-filled for us today as for every other generation. Our meditation will lead us gently but insistently from the concrete circumstances and life of Christ in history, to his abiding presence among us not only in the Sacraments, but in the Body of Christ which is the Church. We learn there to love the cosmic Christ, the eternal Word.

The consequences of the Incarnation are vital for us. Throughout the liturgical year we have opportunities to deepen our understanding of what Our Lord did to save us from our sinfulness and restore us to intimacy with the Father. The very fact of the Incarnation means that all that is human has been touched by the divine, except of course for sin. Thirty years of Jesus' life were spent leading the ordinary life of a person of his day in Nazareth. Those days were precious in the eyes of his Father and so were all the activities of Jesus; each one of value, human acts done by one who was God. Thus all our actions, especially in virtue of our Baptism, have a special value in the eyes of God.

A Sense of Wonder

※

None of us will ever be able to fathom completely the meaning of the Incarnation. I often reflect that it is better to kneel humbly and devoutly at the crib and wonder prayerfully about the fact of Our Lord's birth. Better that than to try to understand fully with the power of our own minds the truths of our faith.

Is it not the case that in our day people do not easily admit, and accept, the limitations to their understanding of the great truths of our religion? There is a pride of the mind which rejects what it cannot understand and denies what it cannot prove. How important it is to recognise that faith begins when reason can go no further. It is faith that enables us to see in the child in the crib, not just a child, but him of whom St John wrote: 'The Word was made flesh and dwelt amongst us.' Not to believe is a modern disease.

St John speaks in a way that is hard to understand. In the early Church he was often referred to as an eagle, one who could fly higher than the others, and so see things differently. But we have to listen to him, even if we find it hard to follow, because all the words of

Scripture were written for us, to help and guide us. St John is trying to take us right into the secret life of God himself, to where the child we see in the crib really belongs: outside time, outside space, outside this world. That child lying in the crib, small and helpless, belongs of course to Mary and Joseph. He is their son, born of her, part of her flesh. But before that, and everlastingly, he is God's Son, his own Son.

I am sure you find it hard, as I find it hard, to keep up with St John when he writes about that perfect Word. The eagle has soared too high and we are left behind, grounded, as it were, because our horizons are too limited, earthbound. What is more, and very significant, our minds are also wounded because of the sinful condition we all share. When we cannot believe it is a sign of our being wounded.

Society becomes sick when it cannot believe, and does not believe because it is ailing. Society in general, and we in particular, only begin to get better when we ask for help. No one can believe without help, and help is not given, normally, unless it is asked for. It is the humble who see the need and make it theirs.

When we have done what the shepherds did, watched and prayed, then we shall be able to raise our minds to where the eagle flies, and share his vision.

The Choice between Mystery and the Absurd

🌿

He told me how many a night he had tossed and turned in his bed, his mind disturbed, anxious and depressed. The death of the one he loved most, his wife, the business he had started near collapse, the pain that heralded the beginning of his last days, at least so he feared. He could not understand why it had to be like this, the pains that are part of life. Darkness in the mind, no purpose, no meaning, the futility of it all. Life is absurd, so he had once read, quite absurd. We are but playthings tossed here and there by the gods, who delight in their callous games.

He had gone in search of a clue, but none could he find. He had heard of one who had come as a Saviour, one who had been born in a manger nearly two thousand years ago. He was vulnerable and weak like the rest of us, though he had enjoyed certain miraculous powers, they said. 'I want my pain removed, my broken heart mended, my anguish taken away,' he prayed, but there was no answer, none at all. He would pray no more, for there was no one to listen, no one to heal, only pain to be endured, stoically, accepting the inevitable. And when it was all over, what would there be? Anything or nothing? He was looking into a dark bottomless pit of misery, or so it seemed. If life is absurd then surely, he reflected, to be destined for nothingness when death comes was folly indeed, the ultimate in absurdity. Are absurdity and nothingness our destiny?

He came and spoke to me. 'How am I to think? My prayers are not answered, I have nowhere to go. I cannot find the answer to life's riddles. Are there any answers?' His voice was plaintive, pleading even. I paused for a moment and thought. Then I said: 'I will tell you a story. Whether it is true or not, I do not know. It happened thus.'

They were all lined up, ill clad, some not dressed at all, men, women and children too. They would walk a few yards, no more, for the gas chambers were close at hand. A child sobbed – a gypsy girl, I believe – and she hung on to her doll, grimly. She had nothing else, nothing at all. An old man tripped and fell, a blow from a rifle-butt sent him once again to the ground as he staggered up. One of the guards looked on, idly at first, uninvolved save to shout an order from time to time. Then he looked at them going two by two into the gas chamber. A soldier tried to snatch the doll from the weeping child, but she hung on. In that moment, the guard who was watching began to change. The hardness of his heart softened, he felt ill at ease, the streak of cruelty within him was no longer his master. He felt shame, only shame. 'What am I doing?' he asked himself. 'What have these people done to be treated like this? It should not be.' What could he do? Rush to save them? Fight off the other guards? No, he would join the throng walking into the gas chamber. He would become one of them, share their fate. He flung his rifle to the ground, stripped off his clothes, and walked to his death, with the old man and the child with her doll.

This is what God did, I told my friend. He stripped himself of his divinity, so to speak, emptied himself and joined us in our pains and bewilderment. I went on with the story:

When the soldier joined the queue of those making their way into the gas chamber, he walked with the child, who held his hand, her other hand hanging on to the doll. The child smiled – serene and at peace. They walked on, side by side, giving strength to each other.

Together they had triumphed over death and over evil, and found the paradox of death leading to life. Christ could have removed all our pain, but chose not to do so. We do not know why. He chose another way. He would walk with us, hand in hand, travel the same road, endure the same trials. Why he did this, we do not know. God's ways are not our ways.

This, however, I do know. His way up the hill called Calvary was burdensome indeed. The load he carried weighed heavily on his shoulders. He fell more than once, was goaded onwards by an unthinking and brutal soldier. As he walked he was sharing our pain, our perplexities, our darkness. Over the hill called Calvary, beyond the tomb, was life. The gas chamber, the little gypsy girl's tomb, had become the gateway to a better and different life.

My friend left me. I went to the crib to pray for him; to pray that where there had been darkness in his life, now there should be light; where despondency and depression, now serenity and hope; where turmoil, now peace. The tragedies in his life would still be the burden he must carry, but the cross would be lighter now and life would have meaning and purpose.

As I approached the crib a child stood there, just looking, in her right hand a doll, tightly held. I watched her, fascinated, awed even. I heard her say, 'Thank you, Jesus'. Then I saw her no more.

The Pilgrim's Dream

❧

It had been a busy day and a bad one. Not that he could blame the people he worked with, nor indeed anything at home. But increasingly something had been nagging him. He could not understand exactly what. True, he was no longer young; his minor health problems could be heralding worse to come. This made him even more ill-at-ease, irritable at home, ineffective at work. Yet there was something else. It was to do with the future, not just next year and beyond. It was the thought that there would inevitably be an end to his life. No one escapes. His achievements were there for all to see; success had been a friend and his bank balance was healthy enough. But where was all this leading?

That night he tossed and turned in bed. Sombre thoughts have a way of gripping the mind and not letting go. When darkness descends, fear takes over. Judgements about people and events are not to be trusted. It was thus with our friend. Then, when exhaustion took over, sleep came. He dreamt.

This was his dream. He found himself walking along

a country road. He didn't know where it came from or where it would lead. There was no one about, no sign of life. He knew that he was lost. After a while he was joined by another traveller and the two of them walked on together. The stranger carried a large book under his arm. Our friend was intrigued. He asked the stranger to tell him what the book contained. The stranger said, 'It tells of an ancient people in a far-off land. Once they had been slaves and then they became free. The book is full of promises, especially about One who would come to do good. In his kingdom justice, peace, true love and respect for life would prevail.'

In his dream the man recalled having heard stories from this book, the Bible, when he was a boy. Its impact then had been minimal – fairy tales, and no more, he thought. Now the stranger sat down by the roadside and began to read. Our friend continued on his way. But he remembered later how his heart had warmed when the stranger had spoken about a man who had died cruelly, and then, it was said, had come back to life.

Come back to life? He couldn't believe such a thing. People do not die and then live again. If you consult eminent scientists and learned scholars of our day, they will tell you that such a thing is impossible. 'Produce the evidence,' they will say. 'Do not be deceived by such a childish message. Ours is a mature age. There is nothing we cannot do or know. What we do not know does not exist.' How often had he heard such talk. He agreed with it. He was, after all, a sensible man. He had grown out of religion.

In his dream he was thinking this when he stopped by a large building. He wandered in without quite knowing why. It seemed to be the church at the end of his street. He didn't usually enter any church, even at Christmas. He thought they belonged to another, darker age of superstition. What good had religion ever done, except to set man against man? Nonetheless, he went inside. He felt ill at ease, furtive, unsure of himself in so strange a place. The church was large and softly lit. He passed an old man sitting at the back, not at prayer but fast asleep. He had no other place to lay his head. Here it was warm and light; outside it was dark and cold. The old man was at home here.

He made his way up a side aisle until he reached a small chapel where there was a crib. He looked at the figures, a woman and presumably her husband, a few shepherds, and a baby lying on some straw. Kneeling by the crib was a child, a girl of about seven. He asked her, 'Who is that baby?' The little girl looked at him, half in pity, half in amazement, at such a foolish question. Didn't he know that this was Jesus? How many Christmases had he celebrated? 'That's Jesus,' she answered. Then she added, 'He's special. He's God.'

Our friend felt irritated by the child's certainty. Yet he had a sneaking feeling that the child knew something he did not. And what about those men and women at prayer around him? They looked sane enough, at ease with themselves and at home in this church. He secretly envied them.

In his dream he the left the church and continued along the road. Still dreaming, doubts and darkness descended once more upon him, joined by their sinister companion, depression.

No, there was no God. There was nothing to life except what this world can offer. He would, he supposed, continue to try to escape from the present moment, fill it with some trivial distractions. He admitted that this did not bring true peace or happiness. Moreover, he knew, deep down, that every pain, every suffering asked the same question: what is the meaning and purpose of life? From that question there was no escape. He walked on, despondent, confused, fearful.

The road ahead was very unclear, for a great mist had descended. Each step was even more faltering than before. Then dimly through the mist he thought he could see the outline of a figure walking towards him. The figure drew nearer. He carried a shepherd's crook in his right hand. He approached our friend and then stopped in front of him.

Later our friend would speak about this extraordinary moment in his dream. It was the eyes of the shepherd that struck him most. 'They seemed to penetrate into the very depth of my being,' he said. 'They were not eyes that were hard and angry, but eyes that were understanding and loving, though not soft and weak. They looked at me and I knew that he respected me and wanted my friendship.'

Then the shepherd spoke: 'I came to look for you, for you were lost, and since you meant so much to me I would even have left other sheep to go in search of you, the lost one.' Our friend asked the shepherd to show him clearly the way ahead. But the shepherd replied,

'No, I want you to live on in darkness, since to show you everything clearly might make you think that you needed no guide, that you were self-sufficient. There is nothing more dangerous than pride, nothing more destructive. For a time you will live as in a fog. You will only be able to take one step at a time. The future will not be clear, nor the way into it. But we shall walk together side by side, and soon we shall reach our Father's house – yes, my Father's and yours.'

Our friend woke up. For the first time for a very long time, he knelt down to pray, and this is what he said: 'Lord, I do believe. Guide me in the way of your love.' Yes, Christmas was going to be different this year, quite different. Now he understood.

Later that day he took his children down the street to the church he had visited in his dream. He felt surprisingly at ease going inside. He showed them the crib. He explained to them that the child in the manger was God made man. He knelt with them. On the way out he saw an old man wrapped in a soiled blanket, sound asleep in a corner. He went over, gently placed some money in his jacket pocket, and crept silently away.

The Third Millennium –
A Challenge

To embrace the Mystery
Is to discover the real.
It is to walk towards the light,
To glimpse the morning star,
To catch sight from time to time
Of what is truly real.

Will Our Society Seize the Opportunity?

Salt and light

'You are the salt of the earth . . . You are the light of the world.' (Matthew 5:13, 14). Those words were addressed by Jesus to his disciples. But are those the only disciples? Clearly, no: because the words Our Lord spoke at a specific moment in time, and in a particular place, were for all time to his disciples in every age. So those disciples clearly include you and me. The words he said then continue to echo through the ages. If you call out in a mountain range sometimes the voice will repeat and repeat. That is as near as I can get to an illustration of how the words of Christ on a particular occasion echo down the ages – the same voice, the same message.

The words were of course recorded by the evangelist, but there is far more than an historical record in the words of Christ when they are solemnly proclaimed Sunday by Sunday or day by day in a very special way. Each word of Christ is relevant to each one of us and is contemporary and personal. So we should never listen to the words of Christ in the Gospel as if they were something from the past and no more, but rather as something for the present and for us now.

So what is Christ saying to you and to me? He reminds you as he reminds me that 'You are the salt of the earth'. Think for a moment about that: you are the salt of the earth. But what if the salt loses its flavour and becomes useless, no good but to be thrown away? Without salt a dish or a bowl of soup is boring and dull, unpalatable. A Christian can become as 'salt without savour' and so become dull and uninteresting. That is a thought to remember.

He also tells us, 'You are the light of the world'. Gracious me, do I see myself as the light of the world? Who has spotted me during this last week as reflecting in some marvellous manner the light of Christ? Not by anything dramatic or by being particularly different from other people, but just in there being something special about me, something other people notice. For some of you, when you were baptised a lighted candle was handed to your sponsor to remind everyone that you have to be like a light of Christ in whatever society you find yourself.

Have you hidden that little light you received in Baptism, or are you trying to be the light of Christ in the world? In other words, to put it more bluntly – and a question I ask myself – how committed am I as a Christian to being a disciple of Christ? Am I like salt which has lost its savour, or like a light hidden under a tub? Isaiah gave us a hint we can use as a test: 'Share your bread with the hungry, shelter the homeless poor, clothe the naked one you see.' (58:7–10). This is not an easy test for many of us – to share our bread, give shelter to the homeless and clothing to the naked.

The point of these illustrations is to ask: Are you concerned for other people? Are you concerned to make our society a better place for all of us? Not in a great and dramatic way, but rather like the use of salt. We don't see the salt in soup, but we know when it is not there. This should be our role – a quiet influence, an attitude of love.

Another hint was given by St Paul: 'I have not come as a great philosopher, I did not come for great arguments. The only thing I have to offer is Christ Jesus' (1 Corinthians 2:1–5). Then he went on to explain that faith does not depend on human philosophy but on the power of God. We become recipients of that power of God, channels of that power, through our life of prayer and the Sacraments. There are two very clear and obvious tests of how committed we are as disciples: our commitment to the Sacraments and our search through prayer to explore the meaning of God and the love he has for us. Then of course there is also the test of our love of God in our attitude to others.

❦

Reflection on the millennium

I was reflecting recently on the millennium and the kinds of things that are going to take place round about midnight on 31 December 1999, New Year's Eve: the parties there will be, the BBC's plans for marking the event, the gathering in the great dome and the plans for a great explosion of fireworks.

Then I reflected on the fireworks – the colours, the excitement, a symbol of the mood we shall all be in. When the firework has done its job, a charred stick falls to the ground. That is all that is left, a charred stick to be picked up from the gutter. So when the new millennium comes, will that be the only thing left? With the party over, will there be nothing but charred sticks? Or is our society going to seize the opportunity, the moment to become different, so the next thousand years will be different, will be better than the last thousand? I have a terrible fear that the homeless will still be homeless, the unemployed still unemployed, church congregations still diminishing – ghastly things to think about and look at. Business as usual when the parties are over.

But it is we who must change the situation and we will only change it if we change ourselves. Isn't that what the Holy Year is about? Repent and believe the Gospel, become his disciples, committed, different, in order to become truly salt, truly light.

What are you going to do after the parties on 31 December 1999? Will you be different? Will you be like good salt, bright light?

What Is Important to Me?

❧

No servant can serve two masters

The point of the Gospel (Luke:16:1–14) is quite clear. The unjust servant is in great difficulties, but he knew what he wanted and took the necessary steps to get it, and is praised by Our Lord. It is strange, so Our Lord would have us suppose, how clever and cunning we can be when it comes to things of lesser importance, but when it comes to things of first importance then we don't show the same certainty of touch in knowing where we are going and how to get there, what we want and how to get it. The application to ourselves is, I think, self-evident and hardly needs labelling. Suffice it to say that we are to be clear as to what we really want in our lives and we have to plan how to achieve our aims.

That kind of good sense is required in our life with God as much as it is needed in making our way in the world. But there is a stark and rather frightening, and too often neglected, reminder at the end of the Gospel: no slave can be the servant of two masters; he will either hate the first and love the second, or treat the first with respect and the second with scorn.

The sharp distinction between the master which is the world and the master which is God is put forward in this Gospel, and indeed elsewhere, with a rather unsettling emphasis. The point of putting it in this uncompromising way is to force us to ask ourselves the questions: What is really important to me? What do I really want? Where do I think I am going? It is not easy to answer this with honesty, or even to face up to the question. But I have to face it or admit that I do not know. Because a life which is not dedicated and devoted to someone or something will be dull and drab; you might call it cautious or prudent, but it will be diminished and uninteresting.

God must always be behind and beyond the immediate aims which we set ourselves. Our immediate aims must be related, or have reference to, that ultimate aim, that ultimate end of our lives which must be God. An individual life which does not recognise a gradation of priorities is chaotic. A society which fails to keep priorities graded, with the ultimate and dominant being God, will be chaotic.

If you dethrone God, you enthrone man. And if you enthrone man he will soon be dominated by forces over which he will eventually lose control. Power, technology, science can, and indeed may in the end, rule our society. But if God is enthroned in the place which is his due then there is a natural and inevitable grading of priorities. As St Paul writing to Timothy advised: '... there should be prayers offered for everyone –

petitions, intercessions and thanksgiving, especially for kings and others in authority, so that we may be able to live religious and reverent lives in peace and quiet' (1 Timothy 2:2). It is advice we should ponder and follow ourselves if our society is looking for peace and tranquillity, a true religious and reverent way of living in which the priorities are established and clear – and at the top there must be God.

Today, in a very special manner, we need both in our public life and in our private lives to reassert the scale of values. Because if we do not, we shall be imprudent people, less astute than the children of this world, and shall fail as the children of light.

God and the Future of
Our Society

❧

A society still searching for purpose

What might a clear-eyed and unbiased visitor notice as she travelled through our society observing people at home, at work and in their relationships? She would see a world of sharp contrasts.

The rush and business of life would strike her. She would be amazed at the rapid growth of computer power, the global horizon opened up by satellite communications. She would watch the faxes and mobile phones, computers and Internet. She might ponder the wisdom of a society whose unrelenting demands for instant communications and entertainment through the media seemed to leave little room for personal reflection and stillness. She would find that many older people were living alone or being cared for in nursing or residential homes. She would see too that medical advances were enabling people to live longer and also raising ever more complex ethical questions as death approaches, noting that some people were arguing for the introduction of euthanasia.

Our visitor might conclude that she had visited a society steeped in history, rich in achievement and blest with extraordinary potential, yet one that is ill-at-ease with itself, offering so much but full of doubts and contradictions, a society still searching.

If our visitor happened to meet me at this point in her journey, she might begin with a provocative question, such as: 'Are you not presiding over the terminal decline of a bygone faith?' Or she might ask: 'Are we not living in a post-Christian or even a post-religious world in which Christianity is scarcely visible any more?' I would take her into a bookshop and show her the astonishing proliferation of titles on astrology, the paranormal and New Age thinking. She would see that many people have a thirst to find out about contemplation and the disciplines of the Eastern religions.

Very many people today are willing to admit to being 'spiritual', even if far fewer would call themselves religious. This is to be expected in a post-Christian country where for many the externals of institutional religion may at first seem alien, yet who find within themselves desires and longings which they cannot satisfy. As the psychologist Carl Jung pointed out, in essence it is a spiritual quest on which people seeking therapy are engaged.

The validity of religion

I believe that the human heart is naturally seeking the ultimate meaning and purpose of life. It is a religious quest. Each person is a naturally religious being. As Archbishop Ramsey once wrote: 'There is a space in every person which only God can fill.' There is much that points to the truth of religion. The witness of martyrs prepared to suffer and die for their faith has been compelling in every age, including our own. I would tell our visitor of the experience I had of meeting a man who had been in an Albanian prison for 43 years because he was a Catholic priest. I knelt before him, a frail, bent man of 94, who by his witness had been a candle in the dark and whose spiritual and moral authority blazed in the light.

There are those of all faiths and none who by their selfless dedication to serving the needs of others, challenge the way we live today. We can see people who devote themselves to the service of others in response to the call and example of Jesus. Mother Teresa of Calcutta was one such person, and there are countless others. These are many of the saints of our day, living out the Gospel command to love in hard, tiring and unrewarding lives dedicated to selfless care for others.

❦

The need for stillness

Our visitor has seen a society hurtling through life,

reluctant to stop, unless forced to do so. Now, more than ever, we need to slow down and be still. Especially in moments of despondency, suffering and stress we need to continue our search for God, away from the business of life.

It is in silence and stillness that we hear the voice of God calling us to look for him in the world he has created, and to listen to his voice speaking deep within us. An Old Testament passage springs to mind, where God is found not in the hurricane nor in the earth-quake, nor in the fire, but in the sound of gentle stillness (1 Kings 19). To be silent and still is an art to be learned. It has its own discipline and difficulties but the learning of it is essential lest we be trapped in the purely secular and the material. Experience shows that silence and stillness open us up to dimensions beyond the immediate. We have to withdraw from time to time to gain perspective, to look beyond this world and to search for the origin and purpose of it all.

※

The life of the spirit

I urge people to look within themselves and ask search-ing questions. The most obvious, and the one that haunts most cruelly, is: 'What happens to me after death?' Do I end up six feet underground or in the furnaces of the crematorium, and does that constitute all that I have been? I am no more. For many of us that is an unsatisfactory answer. The thought that life is ultimately an absurdity is unacceptable, not to say depressing. The will to survive speaks of something stronger.

None of this establishes definitely that we survive after death. Nor indeed does the fact that what we most desire seems to be unattainable in our present human condition. There is a longing deep within each of us for a happiness that is complete and unending, a powerful desire for the best. One of the characteristics of happiness is to love and be loved in a manner that knows no limits, and which cannot be achieved in this life. We reach out to something or someone which is not quite within our reach, just beyond our grasp, the most loving and the most lovable. We have plenty of hints in the experiences of love that we have known, foretastes of what it will be like.

A similar line of reasoning could be developed in respect to truth. We want to know all that can be known. The mind is restless until it is finally in possession of all truth, by which I mean all that is, and the ultimate reason for everything. Mind and heart strive to know and to love. We reach out beyond ourselves for someone whom to know and to love is what we have been searching for all our lives, albeit unknowingly. This can be the beginning of a life in which prayer plays a part. Spirituality has been discovered.

🦋

Vision of the future

My vision is of a society which will nourish the spiritual, in which we each take the time to stop, to listen and to respond to that call of the spirit in our own hearts. We should also ask whether God has ever spoken to us. If so, should we be heeding what he has said?

My vision is also of a society that will look after the weak and the marginalised, promote freedom and nurture an inclusive solidarity based on the dignity and worth of all its members. We are called to express our concern for the poor throughout the world, to do what we can to combat injustice, to express our solidarity with other people.

In this way, through spiritual renewal and social action, we can develop a keener and more vivid awareness that human fulfilment cannot ultimately be found in isolation from the fulfilment of others. We will see more clearly the truth that we are bound together in this world as one family, brothers and sisters. Above all, I share the vision of the present Pope who once declared that the cornerstone of his pontificate was to 'explain the transcendental value of the human person' most visible in the Gospel; and in the free exchange of human love in marriage and the family – love like that of God himself, total, faithful and open to life.

A Sign and Witness

God speaks through experiences

As we approach the second Christian millennium, it is
a time of both opportunity and anxiety. We are in the
midst of radical reappraisal and realignment. Some see
only death pangs while others discern the dawn of an
enriched and better future. Believers in a God who
creates all things out of love are by conviction eternal
optimists. We do not ignore or underestimate the
emptiness, the failures and the pain of our human
existence, but find in them intimations of a God who
redeems and restores.

Religion is an essentially human response. It is to be
found in every culture and at all stages of history. It
remains at the heart of human society as a sign and
witness to the mysterious but real presence of the spirit
and the spiritual in the affairs of every community. The
last two hundred years have seen the absorption of
Christian values into the fabric of our society in many
remarkable ways, but recent years have also seen a
gradual retreat in the public role and influence of

institutional religion. People often say now that religion is, and should be, purely a private matter. It is not so.

Human beings, in all their frailty and limitations, long for the absolute and the transcendent. We have an insatiable hunger for the infinite. It was Chesterton who remarked that when we cease to believe in God, then we start believing in anything. In order to find God we must go in search of him, unless of course he intervenes in a dramatic manner in our lives, as he did in the case of St Paul. His normal mode of coming into our lives occurs when we set out to meet him. As we wander, often uncertainly, generally clumsily, he comes to meet us. He reveals himself in many different ways, and in the most remarkable manner through his Son made man for us. But this is to move into another sphere of experience which we call faith. Religion begins to play a part in our lives when we go in search of meaning and purpose. It is a personal quest and no one can undertake it for another.

It is in the passing of the years that I now look back and realise the significance of what, in themselves, may seem trivial experiences. It is often through such things that God speaks to individuals. So with hindsight I believe that through these experiences God was giving me a hint to look beyond myself and the preoccupations of the world to discover something – indeed, someone.

❧

Death, a prelude to a richer experience

One of my earliest childhood memories was the sight of a coffin being borne through the streets of Newcastle to its final resting place. My thoughts at the time were no doubt childish and unformed. But the incident was a starting point which over the years led to a more mature reflection. Why should death happen? I found that I was unable to believe that death should be the end. It just did not make sense. It could only make sense as a prelude to a richer, more lasting existence.

Many years later I came across a passage from Bede's *Ecclesiastical History* which speaks across the centuries of this same profound human question: why death?

> When we compare the present life of man on earth with that time of which we have no knowledge, it seems to me like a swift flight of a sparrow through the banqueting hall where you are sitting at dinner on a winter's day. In the midst there is a comforting fire to warm the hall; outside, the storms of winter rain or snow are raging. This sparrow flies swiftly in through one door of the hall and out through another. While he is inside he is safe from the winter storms; but after a few moments of comfort he vanishes from sight into the wintry world from which he came . . .

The deepest promptings of the human spirit whisper that there is more to human life than the span of years allotted to it and I began to search for something belonging to a different order of reality which would correspond to this deep intuition that death could not have the last word.

Happiness

When preparing for university examinations at school we were asked to write an essay on a single subject – 'happiness'. What is happiness? Are people generally happy? Happiness struck me then as elusive. Much later I found in St Thomas Aquinas a teacher to guide me in this, as in much else. He argued that we are indeed made for happiness, but the kind of happiness we deeply crave must have two qualities if it is to be satisfying: it must be complete, leaving us with no other desires, and it must be permanent. Something deep inside the human breast is never satisfied in this life and if we are not ultimately to be frustrated, then it is elsewhere and in some other form of existence that we shall find a happiness complete and without end.

The experience of love

It is exhilarating to discover another who will captivate our heart and occupy the empty space within it. It is thrilling to realise that we have a privileged place in someone's heart and life. We discover that love can raise us to the heights, and also plunge us to the depths of despair. But we begin to learn that in some way we are made for love, and that all true human love, however transient and imperfect, has in it something of the infinite and eternal.

One of the most moving accounts of human love I have ever read is given by Viktor Frankl who was in Auschwitz. His wife was also in a neighbouring camp, but they were not able to see each other. He writes of a moment when he was stumbling to work in the icy wind before dawn, when suddenly his wife entered his mind:

> Real or not, her look was then more luminous than the sun which was beginning to rise. A thought transfixed me; for the first time in my life I saw the truth as it is set into song by so many poets, proclaimed as the final wisdom by so many thinkers: that love is the ultimate and highest goal to which man can aspire. I grasped the meaning of the greatest secret that human poetry and human thought and belief have to impart – the salvation of man is in love and through love . . . For the first time in my life I was able to understand the words: 'The angels are lost in perpetual contemplation of an infinite glory'.

'The salvation of man is in love and through love' – few thoughts are more exhilarating than the realisation that 'God is love' and that he has for each person an intensity of love which no human experience of love can match. Human love is nonetheless a wonderful instrument whereby we may begin to explore the meaning of love in God.

None of these experiences proved in any sort of conclusive manner that God existed, yet each one was, and remains, a pointer to another form of life that would persist after death. Each experience carried within it glimpses and a promise of an existence characterised by an unending *now* of ecstatic joy when united to One who is, of all that is lovable, the most lovable of all.

Without God, Life Is Without Meaning

❦

Without God life is ultimately without meaning and thus all too easily becomes inhuman. This meaninglessness undermines freedoms and values essential to our well-being.

Religion, true religion, carries always within itself the seeds of renewal and fresh hope. Genuine religious experience leads eventually to reconciliation and new life. That is for me the fundamental difference between true religion and those ways of thought and action that either impose a narrow religious ideology, or deny the transcendent, and set out to marginalise or root out God from human life and society.

Attempts to render religion irrelevant, or to outlaw it, have multiplied in this century. Destructive regimes have left behind monuments to their inherent evil. I have twice visited the extermination camp at Auschwitz, still one of the most terrifying places on earth – a stark reminder of the systematic and brutal rejection of the values of the Christian faith. It is a moving place in which to be, a place of tragic and poignant memories. In one hut there hangs a picture of young people singing and under it an inscription:

> I freed Germany from the stupid and degrading fallacies of conscience and morality ... We will train young people before whom the world will tremble. I want young people capable of violence, imperious, relentless, cruel ...

The name 'Adolf Hitler' appears below the inscription. These words constitute a complete denial of all that is good and noble.

In Western society belief in God has been massively undermined for nearly two centuries. There has not been a formal assault, but a general acceptance throughout society that unbelief is the necessary consequence of the development of science and a rational approach to the great questions of life. Morality and human values, it is claimed, do not need to be underpinned by a belief in God in a world come of age. Experience suggests that morality in fact does not easily survive, and certainly loses its inner coherence and its values, once it is divorced from faith in a Supreme Being. The decline in religious belief and practice has created a spiritual and moral vacuum, and some despair about finding any satisfying meaning in life. Enlightened self-interest and concern for the common good have failed to halt the spread of materialism and consumerism.

Our century has witnessed an explosion of knowledge both about the world and the universe of which we are a part and about the hidden and all-pervasive inner world which embraces the conscious and unconscious alike. Far from challenging belief in God this knowledge has led to a renewed and deeper awareness of the transcendent. We have been reminded yet again that our abiding temptation is to limit our understanding and image of God and always to make him too small.

⁂

Searching for God

Each individual in search of healing and wholeness is constantly seeking what can only be described as God. Carl Jung, in his book *Modern Man in Search of a Soul*, wrote:

> Among all my patients in the second half of life, that is to say, over thirty-five, there has not been one whose problem in the last resort was not that of finding a religious outlook on life. It is safe to say that everyone of them fell ill because he has lost that which the living religions of every age have given to their followers; and none of them has been really healed who did not regain his religious outlook. This, of course, has nothing whatsoever to do with a particular creed or membership of a Church. (Chapter 11)

The mind will not rest until it is finally satisfied that it has found the meaning and purpose of our human lives. The heart will continue to be wayward, now wanting this, now that, until it possesses that which will totally satisfy it. There is an insatiable appetite in our minds for truth, and in our hearts for love.

❧

The stars only shine in the darkness

Proofs or arguments obscure the truth. How can we discover truth by intuition rather than establish it by reasoned argument? Intuition is that knowledge of an object which does not depend on the laborious process of logical reason. It is instead the impact made by an object or truth on the intellect. It is the sudden and immediate recognition by the mind of something, or indeed someone, other than itself. I liken it sometimes to the objects in a room when the light is turned on. They were there in all their reality in the dark. The eye just recognises what is there when the light appears.

The human intellect can act as if it were a light. Objects are immediately recognised for what they are. At once, too, some of their qualities become evident without the need for demonstration or argumentation. A Dominican theologian wrote: '. . . our intelligence is intuitive. The first act at the dawn of its life, at its awakening, is an intuition . . .' A child's awakening to the reality around it illustrates well the process of discovery and contemplation by the intellect. It has been admirably expressed in a French catechetical document:

[59]

God speaks very gently to children, often without words; the natural creation provides the vocabulary – leaves, clouds, flowing water, a shaft of light. It is a secret language, not to be found in books. One sees a child pause suddenly in the midst of some activity, brought to a silent contemplation of some natural object or living creation or picture . . .

Perhaps intuition is simply the lifting of a veil or the opening of a door to enable the human spirit to enter and possess its proper domain. Just as I cannot conceive that all human life ends in nothingness and futility, so I cannot believe that the beauty of creation is not itself a message, a word of God to lead us into exploration, discovery and abiding wonder.

Faith in the
Contemporary World

꙳

The world, paradoxically despite innumerable signs of denial of God, is nevertheless searching for him in unexpected ways, and painfully experiencing the need of him. The world is calling for evangelists to speak to it of a God who the evangelists themselves should know and be familiar with as if they could see the invisible.

(Evangelii Nuntiandi, Pope Paul VI)

Faith in the contemporary world is not easy. It has two enemies: one is secularism and the other is consumerism. Think about those two, analyse them and it becomes quite clear how they are inimical to faith. I go on reading that because it haunts me. I know that when it comes to speaking of God and the things of God, I am deaf-mute and I don't see clearly.

Happily I have been with people who do see something of the invisible, and have been with people who can speak eloquently of the things of God from their own prayer experience, and that has always been an encouragement and edification. Let me quote two in particular. I remember, just after being appointed to this job, spending forty minutes with Pope Paul VI. I found that an unforgettable experience because I knew I was with somebody who was in an entirely different league. It was, as far as I was concerned, a transforming experience. I found the same with Mother Teresa. These were two people who, in my experience, I felt had glimpsed something of the invisible and were able to talk to the world as if they were familiar with it.

When our faith is not very strong, it is good to spend a bit of time reading those lovely passages in the Gospel where Our Lord is concerned with the blind or with those who are deaf-mute (Luke 18 and Mark 7). I find I am deaf-mute and don't really listen to the Word of God, and I am blind because I don't really 'see the invisible'. So I am unable to express myself to the people of God as they have the right to expect. I need to hear the Word of God,to see the invisible with the eyes of faith. So I pray to the Lord to move me with pity, and to touch my ears so that I may listen, and touch my eyes that I may see, then loosen my tongue that I may speak.

That is the way faith works. You become enthusiastic and love the Word of God even though not seeing in the physical sense the realities being described. But I do see with the eyes of faith, and understand what those men on the way to Emmaus said: 'Did not our hearts burn within us as he talked to us?' Then that wonderful revelation when they recognised him in the breaking of bread. I believe it is often like that. We listen to the Word of God and then it is in the breaking of bread that the understanding comes. How well that describes the two halves of every Eucharist. I once read this from a Greek theologian:

> We see that it is not the task of Christianity to provide easy answers to every question, but to make us progressively aware of a MYSTERY. God is not so much the object of our knowledge as the cause of our WONDER.

What are the Articles of Faith to you and me? They are pointers to the mystery, entries into the mystery. They are starting points for endless exploration, right down the ages, and that exploration is never completed, either by the Church itself or by us individually.

❧

Doubts

'Lord, I do believe. Help thou my unbelief.' What a marvellous prayer that is. I used to confess from time to time to sins of doubt, until I realised that doubt was my friend and not my foe. Doubt is the instrument to purify my faith. It is only when I begin to doubt that I really make an honest act of faith. Time and again it is against all the odds, against everything my brain is telling me. But faith must always be purified, again and again, because it is the purification of faith that leads to charity.

If you have doubts, try to understand that this can

lead you to make that perfect act of faith which is always done in pain, and sometimes in agony, but leads in a most remarkable way to peace and serenity. Why? Because, as we all know, faith is a gift from God.

Changing Hearts and Minds

❦

We are living at a time of profound change and uncertainty. Economic development and technological advances are transforming society at an ever faster rate, and the gulf between rich and poor grows apace. So as we approach the threshold of the third millennium there are many signs of hope, but also reasons for fear.

There is, I believe, a yearning in many people for a moral and spiritual renewal to restore respect for truth and to rebuild trust. In societies like ours, where freedom of choice has been too often elevated into an idol, the rediscovery of shared moral and spiritual values is essential if democratic freedoms and even the fabric of law and order are to be preserved.

The task is a formidable one. It involves nothing less than a transformation of our culture. By 'culture' I mean the sum total of those values which determine our ways of thinking and acting. Many of the values prevalent in our society are too self-regarding and very materialistic. If such attitudes are to be transformed, then minds and hearts must undergo profound changes.

This task, in which the Church has a very important part to play, involves appealing to our common humanity. It means proclaiming the sanctity of human life – the unique value of every individual, and the interdependence of all human beings. It means proclaiming the inviolable rights of every person and their responsibilities, and protecting those who become vulnerable through illness or disability or old age. It means escaping from a mentality which sees society just as a mass of individuals placed side by side without any concern or responsibility for one another. It means embracing instead a vision of the common good, a culture which gives priority to bringing about those social conditions which will best serve to promote and protect the dignity of all.

In 1933, as the Nazi threat was taking shape, Christopher Dawson wrote these words with, I believe, true prophetic insight:

> In fact, the great tragedy of modern civilisation is to be found in the failure of material progress to satisfy human needs. The modern world has more power than any previous age, but it has used its new power for destruction as much as for life; it has more wealth, yet we are in the throes of a vast economic crisis; it has more knowledge, and yet our knowledge seems powerless to help us. What our civilisation lacks is not power, wealth and knowledge, but spiritual vitality, and unless it is possible to secure that, nothing can save us from the fate that overtook the civilisation of classical

antiquity and so many other civilisations that were powerful and brilliant in their day.

Now the need is even more urgent. The first objective is the need to inculcate and foster a personal spiritual life. By that I mean the process whereby God touches both mind and heart and awakens in us an awareness of him and a desire for union with him.

There has to be the expectation of finding God in all things. Our five senses are windows through which the glory of God enters into our inmost being. He is encountered in our every exploration into the worlds of science, nature, history, the arts, and literature. This experience and knowledge has to be interpreted and integrated by the deep study of the Word of God which should form the heart of an imaginative and creative programme of religious education. At the heart of every religious programme must be prayer. Teaching the young how to pray is both profoundly educational and spiritually invigorating.

Today's secular world promotes the view that conscience has merely to do with acting as one sees fit. Individuals are thought to be free to pick and choose the precepts and commandments they observe, as if morality was entirely a matter of choice and opinion. In these circumstances, and in spite it being unfashionable to do so, it is more important than ever to underline the objectivity of moral norms and the need to be guided by them.

It is, of course, one thing to uphold moral values and to reach a coherent private and public morality, and quite another to commend this to young people and help them to make these values their own. We have to demonstrate at all times the necessary link between a moral life and a life that is worth living and is both fulfilling and genuinely human. The first disciples began to follow Jesus because they were attracted to him. Goodness is attractive and in fact deeply compelling. We must encourage that inner movement from 'doing the right thing because I ought to' to 'doing the right thing because I want to, and understand why'.

The threshold of the third millennium is a fitting time for reflection and preparation, a moment to dwell on the challenges which face us as Christians in living out the Gospel. The coming of the Holy Spirit in the Church is a permanent gift which gives life to the Church and makes its witness possible. Pentecost is now, and always. This is the ground of our faith in the future, in the possibility of renewal and transformation, and an inspiration for us to play our part, here and now, in building the Kingdom of God.

The Light of Faith

❦

... on those who live in a land of deep shadow, a
light has shone. (Isaiah 9:2)

I think that as pilgrims through life, we are too often
dazzled by the artificial lights of this world, with an
unruly and uncontrolled desire so often for wealth,
for comfort, for fame, for power, for pleasure. All of
these can, no doubt, be good servants. But if we allow
them to become our masters and ourselves their slaves,
then they only deceive and disappoint.

There may come a point when we pause and ask ourselves: are these the only values that matter – wealth,
power, fame and the rest? Do they really bring the
happiness for which our hearts crave? They do not, and
this we discover by experience. When we begin to look
in earnest for those things that will give us deep and
lasting joy, we can become quite perplexed – indeed, at
times rather lost. We move, as it were, into the world
which angels inhabit, God's world – awkwardly, our
ears unattuned to listening to God's Word, our eyes
blind to finding him in what is true, good and beautiful.

But if we persevere in prayer, listening, looking and waiting, then new convictions are born within us, and a new understanding of the things of God. It will be good if the words from the prophet Isaiah may be applied to all of us:

> The people that walked in darkness has seen a great light. On those who live in a land of deep shadow a light has shone. (Isaiah 9:2)

This 'great light' is no artificial one, for it comes from God. Not only does it give light to our minds, but also warmth to our hearts. That light is faith, that warmth charity or love. Both are wonderful gifts from God.

To whom, then, is the light given? It is to those who are humble enough to recognise the limitations of the human mind, to those who realise their need for one to save them from their sins, to those who persevere in their search for God.

How do we begin to become aware of the warmth in our hearts? When does the love of God begin to take over the mastery of our lives? It is surely when we recognise the power and intimacy of God's love for us. It may be a sudden realisation, or it may be the result of years of faithful prayer and obedience to God. But note, above all, that it was love which was the reason for Christ coming among us:

> God so loved the world that he gave his only Son that whoever believes in him should not perish but have eternal life. (John 3:16)

Do you sometimes wonder whether indeed you have

love for God in your mind and heart? Don't fret about that, just remember the simple truth: God is in love with you. That is an astonishing thought. If that thought now begins to be part of your thinking, then you will change and so will your life. You will find that peace which nothing can take away from you.

The Good Shepherd

❧

Man is in search of God, but only because God is in search of man. It is always that way round, for in every case and at every moment the initiative is always his. In Jesus Christ God comes in search of us, like a father seeking a wayward son, like a shepherd risking the ninety-nine to go in search of the one who is lost. It is a search which begins in the heart of God and culminates in the Incarnation of the Word of God. It is a search that is never abandoned, as God seeks constantly to come more fully into our lives. The shepherd never abandons his sheep.

❧

The Prodigal Son

Out of the many texts of Scripture that we could select to talk about God's search for man, there is one which is deeply moving: the story of the prodigal son. It comes in the fifteenth chapter of St Luke's Gospel, a chapter which is about God's search for man expressed in three stories – the good shepherd leaving the ninety-nine sheep to look for the lost one, the woman who had lost a coin and swept the house until she found it, and then the story of the prodigal son, and within that story I would like to quote just one verse. The son had decided to return to his father and we read:

> While he was yet a long way off his father saw him and took pity on him. Running up, he threw his arms round his neck and kissed him. (Luke 15:20)

Can anything be more moving, more consoling, than that little scene, which speaks so eloquently of the way God sees and understands each one of us? Just think of those words. But it is all the more moving when we remember the authority of the one who told us that story – Jesus Christ himself who came to reveal to us the hidden secrets about the Father. The Father is in search of us always, his wayward sons and daughters. Wounded though we are, lost though we often seem to be, mistaken many a time in the way we should search and serve, nonetheless we come back always to that question Peter put to Our Lord: 'Lord to whom should we go? Thou hast the words of eternal life.'

It is in Christ that we find unlocked for us the mystery of God's love. 'Lord, let us see the Father' Philip said, and Our Lord answered: 'He who sees me sees the Father.' So how precious, how important, how wonderful is each word ascribed by the Gospel to Jesus Christ, and how precious and significant his actions. Every word that he spoke, every action he took had something to say to us, something to give. At the very centre is Christ Our Lord, for he is the way to understanding something of the mystery of God.

❦

The Lost Sheep

Lost – it had become tangled up in the briars, a prisoner unable to escape. The mist that hovered over the sheep now became a dense fog. Fog hides the reality which it envelopes, falsifies judgement, compounds loneliness, begets fear. Lost, cold, in despair, such is the waking nightmare of the one who strays from the fold, lives greedily with no thought for others, turns its back on the shepherd.

Then in the distance, still far away, a voice is calling. Not just any call, but naming the one being sought. The shepherd is seeking, calling. The calling of a name is personal. It is the beginning of intimacy. Still held captive by the briars, hidden from the shepherd's vision by the fog, the sheep can only wait. The voice is clearer now – not shrill, or compelling, but inviting response if response could be given. Hope is born, escape possible, freedom close. The joy of being found is exquisite indeed. To be freed from the briars and carried on the shoulders of the shepherd, and to join the flock where the pasture is rich and the hired man held at bay, there peace and joy are to be found. The hired man offers other pastures, dangerous ones, where greed, selfishness and cruelty reign – briars that entangle those who have been deceived and misled. It is otherwise with the good shepherd. He will lay down his life for the sheep, when the hired man will not (John 10:11–13).

The good shepherd is the one who gives freedom to mind and heart. 'I am the good shepherd; I know my own and my own know me' (John 10:14). The good shepherd calls each one by name. He calls gently, persistently, lovingly. He knows us before we begin to know him. He will leave the ninety-nine to look for the one that is lost; no trouble is too much, no journey too long. Love is ever patient, never gives up on the beloved. It is thus with the good shepherd. If he did not love, he would not seek. St John explains why his search for us is relentless, never ending:

> God so loved the world that he gave his only Son so that whoever believes in him should not perish, but have eternal life. (John 3:16)

Two Great Mysteries:
The Trinity and Corpus Christi

❦

The season of Pentecost is almost a preparation, in a sense, for the two mysteries in the Christian religion that most defy our understanding: the Trinity, and Corpus Christi – the reality of the presence of Our Lord in the Eucharist and all that it means. I think that it is not insignificant that those two feasts occur just after we celebrate Pentecost. They are realities we receive through faith.

❦

The Holy Spirit in the Trinity

How does one understand the Holy Spirit? He is often portrayed as a dove. I personally do not find that image helpful, but the one that does help me is 'the tongues of fire' that came down on the apostles, because this has two aspects – fire gives light and it gives warmth. So I have always seen the Holy Spirit as one who gives light to my mind and warmth to my heart. That is his role. He is the sanctifier, the one who makes us 'tick' inside. He helps me to have inner conviction, faith, and inner desire which is desire for God.

Another way of thinking of the Holy Spirit is as love, the love between two people. What it is that attracts each to the other we do not know, but the result is love. So the love between the Father and the Son is a person. The Trinity is the high point of our faith, and when we come to see God as he is in the beatific vision, what we will see is the Trinity. It is a realm of experience and thinking into which we can only eventually be carried by the Holy Spirit. At present we grope towards it in all kinds of different experiences, but it eludes our limited understanding.

❦

Corpus Christi

In 1989 the Holy Father wrote a letter to mark the twenty-fifth anniversary of the promulgation of the Council Document on the Liturgy. Though the changes in the liturgy which we use now were introduced 25 years ago there are a lot of people who have not accepted them. But it is equally true that the implementing of these changes has not been easy or entirely successful. One of the things we have suffered a bit is our faith in, respect for, and reaction to the presence of Christ in the bread and in the wine.

When the Word of God is proclaimed through the

readings in church, then Christ is present for they are his words, his revealed truth. When the priest stands at the altar or performs the sacramental acts, he is acting in the presence of Christ, or Christ is acting through him. Christ is present in the community, in the Word and in the priest, but above all he is present in the bread changed into his Body and the wine changed into his Blood. It is that act of faith in the real presence of Christ in the Eucharist which defies all our reasoning.

❦

The difference between faith and theology

When I come into a church and see the little red light burning in front of the tabernacle, I go down on my knee and genuflect. Why? It is my act of faith in the presence of Our Lord in the Blessed Sacrament. I do it because I believe that Christ is truly present there. I genuflect because of my faith. 'How do I believe?' – the brain begins to wonder, and that is theology. I don't believe because I have worked it out, but because I believe, I want to think about it, meditate on it. That is the difference between faith and the reason I use to examine my belief. But if I come into church and automatically and unthinkingly genuflect while still talking to someone, then I am not expressing my faith. The point is that external gestures express our faith and help to strengthen it. That is why signs and gestures are so important.

Very often people say they find it difficult to believe.

What they are really saying is that they are finding it difficult to understand. Belief is one thing, understanding another. You do not believe because you understand. It is not because I have understood that I genuflect, it is because I believe what Our Lord said.

A good illustration of faith can be conveyed in an experience I had when a young monk. I knew a man born blind, who had a passion for cricket matches. I would take him to matches and give him a running commentary. He had never seen what a human being looked like, never seen a cricket bat or ball, yet he loved going to cricket matches. For all he knew I could have taken him anywhere, told him anything, but he trusted me to tell him the truth. That is what faith is: I do not see, but I trust the one who came to tell us of God.

Action of the Holy Spirit

❧

I think many of us have some idea, however crude it may be, of what God the Father might be like – we can have a picture of a father. It is the same with Our Lord, especially if we get to know him and read about him in the Gospels. But it is not easy to have a picture of the Holy Spirit. The very word 'spirit' suggests a difficulty, for a spirit cannot be touched, it has no voice so cannot be heard, and we cannot see it with the eye. As a result, it is difficult to picture the Holy Spirit.

But we know the Holy Spirit especially in the work he does, or rather the work that is attributed to him. When he first came down on the apostles it was as wind and fire. That was the sign of his arrival. We see him of course in the effects he has, especially in the conspicuously marvellous change that occurred in the apostles after he came: from being timid men, they became courageous evangelisers.

After the Holy Spirit came down on the apostles, St Peter preached a sermon containing the message 'Repent and be baptised' (Acts 2:38) and we are told that on that day three thousand people were baptised. They formed themselves into a community which was a true communion, a real relationship between the members who were there, based upon their communion with God. That communion was inspired by the teaching of the apostles, inspired by their coming together in the breaking of bread and by prayer. Every Christian community is characterised by its fidelity to the faith, by celebration of the Eucharist and by being prayerful. It was that coming of the Holy Spirit that formed the Church, and for those who are baptised it is the way we become members of the Church.

❧

Baptism

Our Lord himself was baptised in the River Jordan and gave a kind of seal by his action to this Sacrament. When we are baptised or when we are confirmed, there is no gust of wind, no tongues of fire. All that happens is the sign, made from human words and actions. In Baptism the sign is water. The Holy Spirit is often connected with water because water is cleansing and gives life. Few of us remember our Baptism, but it is the foundation Sacrament which is the basis for receiving all the other Sacraments.

I want to dwell particularly on two aspects of being a baptised person. The first is to be conscious of the enormous dignity there is in being a baptised person:

You are a chosen people, a royal priesthood, a holy nation, God's own people that you may declare the wonderful deeds of the one who called you out of darkness into his marvellous light. Once you were no people, but now you are God's people. Once you had not received mercy, but now you have received mercy. (1 Peter 2:9–10)

That describes each one of us – a specially chosen person, very precious and always loved with a tremendous intensity on the part of God.

When we are baptised we are anointed, and given a white robe. These are to describe in a wonderful way the dignity which is ours. The old English word 'christen' is a helpful word. When I christen a person I make them like Christ. When Our Lord was baptised in the Jordan a voice came from heaven saying: 'This is my beloved Son, in him I am well pleased.' So it is when we are baptised, that same voice speaks: 'In him, in her, I am well pleased.' When God the Father looks down on us, he sees in us the likeness of his Son. To be christened is to be made like Christ. We can of course spoil that by deliberate, conscious breaking of God's law. But we can always, as you know, retrieve that likeness to Christ by the Sacrament of Reconciliation. The dignity of each one of us baptised is something that we always need to respect, always need to treasure – every one of us living out in our own way the life of Christ, and in so doing, giving honour and glory to the Father.

With that dignity goes responsibility. There comes a

point in Baptism when the father of the child is presented with a candle. The candle is enormously significant because it is a reminder that the person being baptised now has the responsibility to be the light of Christ in the world. We remember that particularly on Holy Saturday night when, after commemorating the passion and death of Our Lord, we prepare to celebrate his resurrection. We repeat our baptismal promises and light a little candle from the Paschal candle, which represents Christ, so that we can carry the light of Christ into the world in which we live.

As we prepare for the celebration of the Holy Year, we must emerge from it different people. There has to be an enthusiasm for the Gospel. There has to be a purposefulness about our involvement in the society in which we live. We have to change in order to be able to change our society. A small candle can make a great deal of light in a dark, cavernous area. A little light can make a difference, many little lights a great difference.

How truly do I live out my baptismal promises? Do I really renounce Satan and all his works, or do I compromise a bit with the darkness of the world, with the secularism of the world? Do I genuinely live out my act of faith which goes with Baptism? Do I try to learn more about my faith? Do I try to deepen my understanding of my faith? Do I find that it leads me to prayer? Does my faith lead me to explore what God is like, to wonder constantly what he is like? Exploring God in and through prayer is a habit which we can acquire. It means stealing a few moments out of the day to be alone with God, to think of all the lovely things we admire, to reflect on all the experiences of love which have been ours, and to see that all these are hints of the lovableness of God, of the beauty which God is.

❧

Confirmation

We are given a candle at Baptism to remind us to be the light of Christ in the world, but that candle often tends to get a bit weak. It flickers and flutters feebly, and especially during adolescence when we really begin to wonder whether we are going to commit ourselves to follow Christ. So the Sacrament of Confirmation becomes, as it were, a kind of booster to Baptism. As a Sacrament, Confirmation may 'go to sleep' and in many people it does, but it can come back to life, be vivified. This can be done by consciously thinking back to the Confirmation we received and asking the Holy Spirit to come once again and play a part in our lives.

When the Holy Spirit first came down on the apostles there was 'a gust of wind and tongues of fire'. The sign now is different, much simpler and more practical: just the sign of the cross made with oil on the forehead of the candidate and the words 'Be sealed with the gift of the Holy Spirit'.

I find myself thinking much about those tongues of fire, especially this last year before the third millennium. I think of a human life in which God plays no part, a life which deep down is cold and dark. I think there must be darkness and coldness in a person who does not have God in his or her life, and I think they try to escape that darkness by looking for warmth in all kinds of different places and different people. A world or a society without God can be cold, uncaring, dark and bewildering.

So we see how important it is for the Holy Spirit to come into our own personal lives and into our society for 'where there is darkness he will give light, where there is coldness he will give warmth'. Those tongues of fire bring warmth to the heart and light to the mind: light, to be able to understand just a little bit more about God; warmth to our hearts so that we can begin to experience a real desire for God – a desire to see and know him, a desire to be with him. Indeed, to go beyond that, a desire to love him.

❧

The action of the Holy Spirit in prayer

Reflecting on those wonderful words of Our Lord in St Matthew's Gospel, 'Come to me, all you who labour and are burdened and I will give you rest' (11:28), we think of Our Lord whispering those words into our ear, personal and relevant to each one of us. If I just hear those words or read them, they remain words. But by reflecting on them I begin to see the thoughts they are conveying, then there comes a moment when I can say, 'It is true. He is calling me to come to him burdened by worries, anxieties, difficulties, pain and all kinds of things.' I suddenly realise that those words are addressed to me. When they change from being words to thoughts, thoughts which become embedded in my heart, then *that* is the Holy Spirit at work.

Cardinal Newman made the distinction between notional and real assent: the latter is when you are able to say 'that is true, I want it'. 'Flesh and blood hath not revealed this to you, but my Father in heaven' (Matthew16:17). That is why the role of the Holy Spirit is so important in our lives and in the Church, because he enables us to move into a different spiritual dimension, beyond words, beyond thoughts, into the silence of being present in God's world.

We get there by starting with the words, then we begin to reflect on them, repeating them slowly in periods throughout the day, then through those words we enter into God's silence. That is contemplative prayer. Never forget that each one of us is called to contemplative prayer, which is the meeting of God's silence with our silence, the meeting of our desiring and God's loving. This cannot be done except by the power of the Holy Spirit. We receive the Holy Spirit when we open ourselves up and pray: 'Come, Holy Spirit, fill the hearts of your faithful, kindle in us the fire of your love. Send forth your Spirit and we shall be created.'

The Holy Spirit has to take possession of our minds and hearts: our minds, so that we understand better the things of God; our hearts, so that we become truly engaged in our following of him.

Saints for Our Time

❦

There is a theme which I find realised in both St Thérèse of Lisieux and St Bernadette. The more I think of those two women, the more I think they have profoundly changed our approach to spirituality and to learning the faith. Both were French, both were uneducated. Bernadette could not read or write; Thérèse could read and write but had a very limited knowledge of life. Bernadette was very important in her lifetime but when she died people lost interest in her. Thérèse was totally unimportant during her life but became very important after her death. Bernadette left to the Church a shrine, Thérèse left to the Church a book, *History of a Soul*.

Thérèse lived in the time of Jansenism – a kind of error or heresy, a spirituality based on fear; the idea of the love of God was not in their way of thinking. But Thérèse completely revolutionised that. I once went to pray in the cell where she died, and stayed for a while on my own. On the wall she had scratched the words 'Jesu est mon unique amour' ('Jesus is my only love'), and I found that intensely moving because she was going through a great crisis of emptiness and darkness and had to do that in order to affirm her faith. Her message to the world is that you cannot grow in holiness except through prayer and a certain degree of suffering. It is my conviction that the Lord was saying through her that you cannot be a good missioner unless you are a person who prays and who knows how to accept and cope with suffering. I think that message is very relevant for us today.

Bernadette, who could not read or write, had to postpone making her first Holy Communion because she could not learn the Creed. Yet she had an understanding of what was taking place which went far beyond her technical knowledge of the Catechism. Her great contribution, as I see it, has been to strengthen people's faith. That is the secret of Lourdes.

I think that these two saints were called at a special time in order to give an important message to the Church: Thérèse about spirituality, Bernadette about faith. There is also a modern-day saint – Teresa of Calcutta – who was called to draw our attention to the preciousness of all life, even the most despised. The two things that Mother Teresa was most committed to were the plight of the poorest of the poor and the campaign against abortion.

It seems to me that the Lord selected these two women to teach the Church something very important, and he chose frail women to do it.

Peace

The Son of God came into the world
to bring peace

On Christmas day in 1914, in the first year of the First World War, the soldiers facing each other in the trenches refused to fire. Instead they walked out into no man's land to sing carols, to exchange their rations and cigarettes. It was their tribute to the Child Jesus, the Christ who is our peace. The next year, the military authorities were ready, and when a soldier tried to repeat that Christmas truce he was shot, and by his own officers.

The idea that the birth of the Messiah would bring peace was first expressed by the prophets in the Old Testament, and repeated and preached ever since. Yet how can we go on believing that there is any real truth in that promise of peace? This century has been soaked in blood: two world wars, the holocaust and the horror of terrorism. It is painfully clear that we have totally lost our way.

The peoples of the world cry out ceaselessly for peace. But how can a world like ours find peace, and some release from its pain? There will be conflict and aggression as long as there is injustice and hurt, discrimination and exploitation. As we draw to the end of this century and recall the savage hatreds which still divide communities, it is hard to summon up the hope that lit the first Christmas. Peace is more than disarmament, more than just the absence of war. It is concerned with justice, respects truth and freedom, is radiant with love.

The Pope warned us: either we learn to walk together in peace and harmony, or we drift apart and ruin ourselves and others. This is a question to be put with some urgency to our political leaders, but it also has to be answered by ourselves. Peace is born in the human heart, your heart and my heart. That is why we need, each of us, to make a constant effort to renounce selfishness and to embrace goodness and the love of others.

The world finds no peace because the world refuses to repent and believe the Good News. The peace of Christ will not, cannot, be imposed on an unwilling world. It must find a home first in human hearts. There has to be a radical change of heart, a deep-down conversion, a death to the sinful ways of pride and self-centredness.

This surely is the point of the Christmas season – the celebration of the Incarnation. The Son of God came into our world not in power, but in peace. He took for himself our human weakness. God looked on our misery and came to be part of it. He identified with the outcast, with the sinner, with the victim. When he wanted to reveal his secret to mankind, he simply showed us a child born in a stable, an outcast crucified on Calvary. His only weapon was love and he has handed to his followers their rule of life: to love God with all their hearts, and their neighbour as themselves. Only along this path will we find lasting peace.

Prayer is a part of our search for peace. It opens up our lives to the spirit of God and his guidance. It makes us aware of the needs and sufferings of our brothers and sisters. But prayer is a pledge of action. It involves us first in turning away from greed, selfishness and violence. It urges us to live the values of truth, justice, love and freedom.

❦

God's love for us

I once had a letter from a lady who wrote this: A man who later became a prominent Christian said how his idea of God was revolutionised when as a little boy he was taken to visit an old lady. The old lady pointed out to him a text on her wall: 'Thou, God, seest me'. She said to him: 'You see those words? They do not mean that God is always watching you to see what you are doing wrong. They mean that he loves you so much that he cannot take his eyes off you.'

I found that letter very helpful and I am sure you and I can find help and reassurance in the image of a God who cannot take his eyes off us. I am sure we need that help, especially as we come to the end of one century and look forward to the next.

[91]

We may be tempted to feel that there are forces outside our control, that the world is lurching from one disaster to another, as indeed it does. But the God who cannot take his eyes off us does not cease to care and be concerned for us. It is we who create so many of the world's problems, and we can resolve many of them with the power and skills that God has given to us.

The eyes of God are on us and they have a longing and a wanting in them for us, for you and for me. He wants us to know and love him, above all things. Our real happiness lies in him and that happiness can begin now, but will only be complete when life is over, and there is a new beginning for us.

We can then face the future with confidence, not because we are strong, wise and successful, but because we have a God who loves us and wants us. All he asks from us in return is that we try to love him, that we try to serve him.

We have to keep our eyes on him.

Silence

❧

The sound of stillness

Silence is a presence of God. It is in this silence that we shall hear a voice deep within us, speaking to our nobler selves, calling us to high ideals and generous instincts. Silence is the voice of God, sometimes no louder than a whisper, but speaking to us unmistakably if we learn to listen, to listen to God. That silence, that presence of God, will bring peace to our troubled and divided hearts. It will help to heal and restore our society.

St Anselm, a monk of a monastery in Normandy and later Archbishop of Canterbury, wrote:

> Come now, turn aside from your daily employment. Escape for a moment from the tumult of your thoughts, put aside your weighty cares. Let your burdensome distractions wait. Free yourself for a while for him. Enter the inner chamber of your soul. Shut out everything except God and that which will help you in seeking him. When you have shut the door say to him: 'I seek your

face. Lord, it is your face I seek. Lord my God, teach my heart where and how to seek you.'

To see God as he is, his beauty and goodness, his power and his truth, to rejoice in the vision of him – for this we are made. It is the purpose of our being, to see the countenance of God, to know his glory.

'No man can see me and live.' But God is gracious. He meets our needs and stoops to help our weakness, to give hints of the glory that is in him. In all that is true, beautiful and good we can find him, if we look, reflect and pray. He gives light to dispel the darkness in our souls. Our senses are windows through which a ray from the glory shines into the inner chamber of our souls.

Like a lover he wants to be closer, to walk with us, to be one with us. So he sent his Son. To see this child in swaddling clothes lying in a manger, is to see God himself – God made man for us. His manhood hides and reveals at the same time the God that he is.

Celebrating the Incarnation – God becoming man – 'we escape from the tumult of our hearts, leave our wearisome toil, and enter the inner chamber of our soul' to listen to his Word: the Word calls us through the mist of ignorance and apathy to be silent, to listen to the sound of stillness and so to see in the child born of Mary, the Word who became flesh.

The Fundamental Truth

In every age, many, too many, had ignored what the prophets had said. So at last God spoke again, in our time, the last days, almost as if it were the last chance, God spoke through his Son: God became man. That is the leap our minds must make. It is the fundamental truth of Christian teaching, a truth which we call the Incarnation.

Either we recognise that truth, or we ignore it as being of little consequence. Sometimes our minds are struck by it and our lives are changed. It is a truth which demands acceptance or rejection.

St John is our guide and he tells us quite categorically that this Son born of Mary is indeed God. He speaks of this Son as a thought or a word of the Father, and then clearly, and with great authority, declares: ' . . . the Word was with God, and the Word was God.' St John, and indeed St Paul as well, lead us into reflecting on the great mystery that God is, what he is like and how he should be the object of our imagination and must command our love. True religion is a search, an exploration, a journey of discovery as we seek to find out exactly what God is like.

St John once wrote quite simply: GOD IS LOVE. These three words are the key to true religion. It is indeed an adventure of love – God in love with you, God in love with me.

The Rule of St Benedict
Its relevance today

❧

I believe that what is to be prized most of all in the Rule of St Benedict is the spirituality that it teaches. Holiness is for all, not for an elite, and we are all called to holiness which is friendship with God and obedience to his will.

The two fundamental duties of the monk are to seek God and to worship him. In fact these are the fundamental duties of all Christians. No human life is as it should be unless God is part of that life. There is something missing in the life of each one of us if we are not in some manner in search of God, this search leading to our recognition of who he is and what we are. In the monastery two aspects of the life are designed to help the monk to make this search for God: spiritual reading, which we call 'lectio divina', and silence.

St Benedict sought silence, solitude, stillness. He became a hermit. Though he may have turned his back on things academic, a hermit acquires a different knowledge and a deeper wisdom. This comes to those who have glimpsed something of God in prayer. It is the knowledge of him as the ultimate truth. It is a wisdom that gives proper perspective to the created universe.

Each of us needs an opportunity to be alone and silent, or even, indeed, to find space in the day just to reflect and listen to the voice of God that speaks deep within us. Ours is a noisy and hectic world. There is too much clamour, too many preoccupations and distractions, so much so that God is squeezed out of our lives, if indeed he had ever been admitted into them. Of course people want to know if there is a God before they seek to admit him into their lives; they want to know where he is to be found, what he is like. Oddly enough it does not always work that way. Very often the starting point is a constant and prayerful search for God. Our search for God is only our response to his search for us. He knocks at our door, but for many people, their lives are too preoccupied for them to be able to hear.

It has always struck me that, unlike us, God does not see or look at crowds. He sees and looks only at individuals: each one the craftsman's handiwork, each one made for a special purpose, each one unique. Our society is inclined to value people exclusively in terms of their skills or income or productivity. As a result, elderly people, or those unable to work, can feel that they are a burden. Such utilitarian considerations do not feature in God's understanding of his creation. God does not judge as we do.

Characteristics of Benedict's Rule

There are four basic attributes required of each monk: that he should truly seek God, be zealous for the work of God, be obedient, and be willing to accept all the difficulties inevitably involved in living for God and in community. Do these characteristics apply only to monks? What about us, you may well ask. It is all a question of vocation. Some of us are called by God to seek him in a monastery, others are called to live in the world, plying all kinds of different trades and bringing up families. It is not a question of one way of life being better or superior. But these four characteristics are among the fundamental principles of every spiritual life – the search for God, the worshipping of him, obedience to his will and the acceptance and embracing of the cross when called upon to carry it.

What if I have no taste to seek God, and much less to worship him? Most of us, though not all, do not pray naturally. We do not go to prayer at first because we wish to pray, but having disciplined ourselves into doing so, we see the need to persevere. This is important when it comes to worshipping in church. We go because we know that it is right. If the music is bad, the language not to our taste, the sermon boring, then we should still go. Why? We go for God's sake, not our own. We have to forget ourselves and think only of him. That is the secret.

The importance of the central truth:
God became man

As humans our knowledge and understanding of God is
severely limited. Although at times we may reach out
towards him, he is always beyond our grasp. Hence the
importance of that central truth: that God became
man. That he did so is a unique claim among all the
religions of the world. In Christ's actions and words we
have translated for us, in a way that we humans can
understand, the truths about God, what he should
mean to us and what we already mean to him. Because
God became man and lived as one of us at a specific
moment in history and at a precise locality, then all
human activities have acquired a new significance. He
who is God lived the life of a man of his time in
Nazareth. There is no secular realm from which God is
absent, where he cannot be found.

Benedict lived at a time of turmoil and instability. In
some respects so do we. Our society reveals a pervasive
uncertainty and anxiety about the future, and a deep
confusion over what is of lasting value. Benedict's
answer was clear: he committed his whole life to God.
In fact, he sowed, but he did not reap. He did not plan
for, or foresee, the extraordinary development of a
worldwide religious order bearing his name. He did not
live to see the full fruits of his labour, which were
enjoyed by the generations who came after him.

The millennium – a challenge

The millennium must be a time for revitalising the moral and spiritual roots of our society. It is a moment for reassessing priorities, individually, as families and communities, and also for the sake of future generations. Moral and spiritual values must first be learned in the home, taught in schools, and a good example set by all of us. The millennium challenge calls for a change of heart and, I believe, one guided and nourished by the God who made us and who loves us.

Handing the Faith on to Children

❦

Teachers as witnesses

> People today listen more readily to witnesses than
> to teachers. If they do listen to teachers it is
> because they are witnesses. (Pope Paul VI, 1974)

Unless the faith means something to the teacher, it will
not mean anything to those who are being taught. The
young, even the very young, are quick to detect
whether or not we are sincere, whether we are honest,
and convinced.

I want to make a very important point. There are
three fundamental truths which must be taught to
children from the earliest age:

1. That God became man, and that Jesus Christ is both
   truly God and truly man.
2. That he is truly present in the Blessed Sacrament of
   the Altar and that it is he whom we receive in Holy
   Communion.
3. That the Mass is not only a meal shared by the parish

community, but is also, and especially, the way whereby we share in Christ's sacrifice to his Father.

I do not believe that children are too young to be taught these truths. It is true that having some understanding of God and his revelation comes later than knowledge. In fact, understanding follows faith; understanding does not lead to faith. It is God's gift of faith that enables us to say, 'I believe'. If we hold, then, that children are unable to accept the truths that I have mentioned, then we may be forgetting the part which the Holy Spirit plays in the act of faith. In my experience children have no difficulty in accepting complex truths. It is adults who find this difficult.

The home, the school and the parish should all work in partnership, for each has a vital and complementary role. But the task of handing on the faith to children is first and foremost the responsibility of parents. Their children are entrusted to them by God. The ways in which God speaks to us of his love – as a Father to his children – is in the language of family relationships. It is not for nothing that the family is called the 'domestic church'. It is the first school of life and love.

Our Lord celebrated the lives of children: '. . . it is to little ones such as these that the Kingdom of Heaven belongs.' (Matthew 19:14). He placed them first and so should we. I firmly believe that there are two vocations which must have pride of place: the calling to be a parent, and the calling to be a teacher. On these two vocations the future of our society rests. Both roles are hard, but deeply rewarding. Both are undervalued, even undermined, in our society. If we really want the best for our children, we must show it in the way we value those who are responsible for bringing them up, and those who teach them.

Prayer

※

At the heart of the celebration of the millennium should be devotion to Our Lord, and prayer. It is important that we meet Christ in the Gospels and in the Blessed Sacrament of the Altar, and that we pay particular attention to the prayerful and reverent celebration of the Mass.

※

Learning to read the Gospel in a prayerful manner

'Come to me all you who labour and are over-burdened and I will give you rest . . .'

As the years go by we become increasingly preoccupied with the question: What is God like? As we walk on our pilgrim way towards the vision of God there are, here and now, hints of what he might be like: words like truth, goodness and beauty. Goodness, which is the lovableness with which nothing can be compared.

Beauty, the like of which could not be conceived in the mind and heart of any of us.

But we need to study Jesus Christ in his Gospels. Reading the Gospels, mulling over the words of Our Lord, turning them over in our minds and hearts, it is there we meet Christ. Whenever Our Lord speaks, pause and reflect that he is speaking directly to you. He is whispering into your ear as you read; that doesn't suggest anything other than the reality of the presence of God in his Word and that he is speaking to you. So when I read 'Come to me all you who labour and are overburdened', I pause, knowing that as I read it I am following with my eyes what I know he is whispering into my mind.

So if we have acquired the habit of reading the Gospels we can build up over the years a number of favourite passages, ones to which we return constantly and find always something new. They are wonderful starting points for our prayer. Remember always that through the idea, through the word, we go directly to the person we are addressing. So over the years, in our spiritual reading – and surely there is no mature spiritual life which does not include spiritual reading, above all the Gospels – we feed our minds and hearts. What is prayer but the raising of the mind and heart to God?

An admirable way of using the Gospel as prayer is to read a passage slowly. Whenever the name 'Jesus' occurs, or 'he' referring to Jesus, change it to you or thou, and change the name of the person to whom Our Lord is speaking to 'me'. In this way your reading of the

Gospel becomes a conversation between Our Lord and you. Is not this what it is meant to be?

The 'prayer of agony' can be ours when we are suffering. I am thinking in particular about times of sadness and sorrow. It may be the death of someone we love very much, perhaps a terrible depression or some other affliction that keeps us awake at night and anguished all day. It is on these occasions that we can make our own Our Lord's prayer in the Garden of Gethsemane: 'Father, if you are willing, take this cup away from me. Nevertheless, let your will be done, not mine.' (Luke 22:42) In other circumstances when, for instance, we feel that all is lost and ourselves too, we can pray as Our Lord did on Calvary: 'My God, my God, why hast thou forsaken me?' (Matthew 27:46). So often when sorely afflicted and sad, it is good just to slip into church and be in agony in the presence of Our Lord in the Blessed Sacrament and try to say: 'Dear Lord, I accept this great pain, or at least I am trying to do so. Give me the strength to carry this cross.'

※

The presence of Christ in the Blessed Sacrament

The Church is nourished and sustained principally by the Word of God, by the Eucharist and by prayer.

By the Eucharist I do not mean only the celebration of Mass, but also our devotion to the Blessed Sacrament of the Altar. A Catholic church is a place where the people of God gather, but it is also a place where Christ is truly and sacramentally present. It is this presence which gives a Catholic church its special character. We must do all we can to enhance our awareness of this abiding presence of Our Lord. We need in the Church today to recapture our devotion to the Blessed Sacrament.

It is a wonderful practice just to sit or kneel in the presence of the Blessed Sacrament, and in a marvellous way a kind of 'presence' begins to reveal itself to us – just being in the presence of the Blessed Sacrament, mind open, heart open, trying to experience something which is unique and which lies beyond our capacity to explain or understand. It requires prayerfulness, it requires humility. It requires us to admit our own deficiencies and limitations, to be able to say in the presence of Our Lord in the Blessed Sacrament: 'I do believe. Help thou my unbelief.' It does work.

We need just to be with Christ and to pray. Some may be as Peter, James and John when Our Lord was transfigured on Mount Tabor: hearts full of admiration and joy. But your mood might be quite different, more at ease to be with him as he was in the Garden of Gethsemane, bringing your pain, suffering and anxieties. Whatever your mood, whatever your concerns, you can in his presence enjoy being with him on Mount Tabor, or suffer with him in Gethsemane. Your mood may be in between those two, a mixture of both. But just being with him, allowing your thoughts and affections to unfurl in prayer in his presence, this will allow those concerns of mind and heart to be blessed and sanctified by him.

Calvary Made Present
in the Mass

❧

I once met a woman who had been in Belsen con-
centration camp for two or three years. She was
remarkable in her looks, in the strength of her face
and the serenity of her expression. She had gone
through that passion and emerged a free woman. She
was totally free inside, and totally peaceful. To me she
was a remarkable symbolic presence of the reality
which is at the heart of the Eucharist, how Our Lord
experienced our pain and gave it meaning and purpose.

I rarely understand that purpose. But suffering and
pain are our human condition and one can only wonder
and reflect on what St Paul meant when he said: 'I
make up what is wanting in the sufferings of Christ.'
(Colossians 1:24). That suffering is symbolised in the
Eucharist. I never cease to be amazed at the extent of
suffering and pain in the world: it is a weighty argument against the existence of God. Yet one has to
reflect on the experience of Our Lord on the cross: 'My
God, my God, why hast thou forsaken me?' He had
lived the reality of those words.

One of my most horrifying experiences was a visit to Auschwitz. It was a most chilling experience to stand in that place with acres and acres of those huts still there, and horrifying to think of the way those people were stripped of their dignity before their lives were taken from them in those gas chambers – stripped so that their clothes could be sold. I thought of Our Lord and how he too was stripped of his robes. Surely that is at the heart of every Eucharist, that pain gathered up by Our Lord. Yet in that passion are the seeds of resurrection and I think of those three words of Our Lord on the cross:

> LOVE: I thirst.
> FORGIVENESS: Father, forgive them, for they know not what they do.
> HOPE: This day you will be with me in paradise.

With the consciousness of love, with the consciousness of forgiveness, with the consciousness of hope, a man or woman can walk through life. Yet it was at the height of Our Lord's suffering on the cross that he spoke those glorious words. So at the heart of Calvary is of course the resurrection. Every time we celebrate Mass, surely all that agony and suffering of humankind is present, and through that offering in some way love, forgiveness and hope are being given – not just to this community round this altar but, like the pebble cast into the pond, the ripples move ever further outwards.

So the Mass makes present that one complete sacrifice of Christ, re-enacted through the consecrated bread and wine, the Body and Blood of Christ, transcending time and space, enabling us to be present at the foot of the cross and close to the empty tomb. It is our earthly way of being involved in the great heavenly liturgy which is going on all the time (Revelation 5:6–14). Our celebration is the earthly counterpart of that liturgy.

The Mass,
Sacrifice and Sacrament

❦

In man's history, the revelation of God's love and mercy has taken the name and form of Jesus Christ. (Pope John Paul II, Redemptor Hominis)

Central to our faith in Jesus Christ, true God and true man, is what he did for us by dying on the cross and rising again to life. It is difficult to understand the great mystery of love which we call redemption. It is a secret, one that is hard to grasp, and then only by the help of the Holy Spirit.

We come closest to that mystery of the redemption when we offer the sacrifice of the Mass, making the offering of ourselves in union with the supreme and eternal offering of Christ in love and obedience on Calvary.

In Holy Communion we are united with Christ and absorbed by him in his self-giving. How important is that precious moment when he is close to us. It is the moment when we must give ourselves to him, as he gives himself to us. It is a very personal time and should not be rushed or invaded by distraction. Moments of silence and stillness after Communion are very important, moments before the final prayer and blessing, and the moments after when we stay behind in church – alone with him.

How much we should treasure the Mass, and how important it is that it should always be celebrated with dignity and reverence, and in a prayerful manner. This is a crying need for the Church to address today, and we have somehow to make the celebration of the Eucharist attractive. We will not do it by making it consciously cheerful, or by eccentric celebrations. We will do it by going deeper into its meaning: that is the secret. We need to rediscover the numinous. That is what the new generation is looking for. People come to our churches because they want to discover God, and they want to go out feeling that they have been touched by him. That is so important. It does not mean changing things dramatically, but I do think that restoring respect for the Eucharist and seeking a sense of the numinous are two urgent needs in the contemporary Church.

❦

The Blessed Sacrament

We need, in the Church today, to recapture devotion to the real and abiding presence of Christ in the Eucharist.

Outside Mass that presence continues and is celebrated through devotion and prayer before the Blessed Sacrament of the Altar. In my view, that devotion was slightly weakened in the years that followed the Council. But we need to rediscover it.

It is an excellent practice just to be in his presence, and allow him to reveal himself to us as we kneel or sit, quietly and alone. That practice will lead us to experience his presence in a very vivid and real way.

The Holy Father wrote in 1980:

> The Church and the world have a great need for Eucharistic worship. Jesus awaits us in this Sacrament of love. Let us not refuse the time to go to meet him in adoration, in contemplation full of faith, and open to making amends for the serious offences and crimes of the world. Let our adoration never cease. (Dominicae cenae 3)

Celebrating
the Incarnation

❧

When you set yourself to look more closely,
You will begin to see some sense
In the darkness that surrounds you.
Your eyes will begin to pick out
The shape of things and persons around you.
You will begin to see in them
The presence of the One
Who gives them meaning and purpose,
And that it is he
Who is the explanation of them all.

The Third Millennium
A New Beginning

❧

We are all privileged to be living at this special time in human history. All over the world Christians are preparing for the sacred year which the Pope has called The Great Jubilee. Under the leadership of Pope John Paul the Catholic Church worldwide is embarked on a journey of repentance and renewal. No new beginning is possible for the third millennium unless we first accept our need as individuals, as a Church and as a society, for forgiveness and healing.

It is of vital importance that we go into the next millennium different people – that is, people intent on justice and peace and aware of that word so often spoken by the Holy Father, with a 'preferential option for the poor'. If we are to become different people, then it is essential that we turn away from what is wrong and evil and turn to God. We have to become men and women who are prayerful, of strong faith and of service to each other. We shall have to strive to ensure that decent values prevail in our society, stress that objective moral laws exist and should be obeyed, object to what is unwholesome or degrading. In short, we must affirm the gift of life and respect the gift of love. Our basic institutions must be alive with zeal for Christ and his Gospel.

Christ is our Way, our Truth, our Life. It is to him that we must turn. After all, the year 2000 is being celebrated to mark his coming into our world – God becoming man, the Incarnation.

I ask you to meet Christ in the Gospels, remembering that each of his words is addressed to each one of us, personally and lovingly. I ask for increased devotion to Christ's true presence in the Blessed Sacrament. I ask, too, that we should make our celebration of the Eucharist prayerful, dignified and reverent.

We must form prayer groups, pray before the Blessed Sacrament, celebrate Mass with great reverence. A change must occur in each one of us if we are to be equipped to play our part as Christians in creating a better society, one to which future generations will be able to look back with gratitude for what we will have achieved. Does this frighten you? Do you find it daunting? I believe that we are called by Christ himself to achieve great things for him and his Gospel. Each one of us is being called.

The Church exists as a sign of union between God and humanity. It is a place for all of us, of welcome, healing and renewal. No one, whatever they have done, is beyond the loving reach of the outstretched arms of Christ on the cross. Our task today is to turn to him who alone can destroy the barriers that separate us from God and from one another.

I am very conscious that there are many baptised Catholics who no longer practise their faith, who may even feel rejected by the Church. There are many reasons for this. I wish to say to those who are distanced from the Church, 'Come back', and to the rest of us, 'Make them welcome'. God does not reject you, nor must the Church. God wants you to turn to him again to learn about his love and to experience it. Your situation may seem impossible. For instance, many will be in second marriages. We cannot change the rules concerning this matter, as you will appreciate. The sanctity of marriage must always be upheld. But help can often be given. There is much the Church can do for you, and you for the Church.

We shall work ecumenically with other Christians. By working with them we can help ensure that the new millennium really will mark a new beginning for our world. I know, too, that in many of the values we hold, we shall be joined by people from other faiths and religions.

I quote from the Holy Father:

> Everything ought to focus on the primary objective of the Jubilee: the strengthening of faith and of the witness of Christians. It is therefore necessary to inspire in all the faithful a true longing for holiness, a deep desire for conversion and personal renewal in a context of ever more intense prayer and solidarity with one's neighbour, especially the most needy. (Tertio Millennio Adveniente, No. 42)

Preparation for the Millennium Jubilee

❧

The Holy Father has called us to celebrate a special Jubilee in the year 2000. Most of all we shall be celebrating the birth of Christ – the day, astonishingly, when God became man and dwelt amongst us.

Like any family or institution celebrating a jubilee we shall want to recall this important event and rejoice in it. Of course we shall enjoy the different secular events organised nationally and locally. But we shall want, surely, to reflect more deeply on the significance of the Incarnation – God becoming man – and, most important, on the consequences for ourselves personally, and for the world in general.

So celebrating the year 2000 should be, must be, a profound religious experience for us all, and we need to prepare for it. How are we to understand the meaning of a Jubilee in the Church?

Two references in Scripture will guide us. First, those words from St Luke's Gospel are very significant, when Our Lord at the beginning of his public ministry read, in the synagogue in Nazareth, some words from the prophet Isaiah:

> The Spirit of the Lord is on me, for he has anointed me to bring the good news to the afflicted. He has sent me to proclaim liberty to captives, sight to the blind, to let the oppressed go free, to proclaim a year of favour from the Lord. (Luke 4:18, 19)

Then he said: 'Today this Scripture has been fulfilled in your hearing.' The year of the Lord's favour had begun.

The author of the Book of Isaiah was writing of the joy of God's people on returning from exile. Increasingly, however, the people were looking forward to the coming of the Messiah. There would come a time when the afflicted, the captives, the blind, the oppressed and broken-hearted would hear good news. Words like liberation, forgiveness, reconciliation and hope describe the good news and the favours to be brought by the Messiah. These words can be called 'Jubilee' words.

The other important passages from Scripture come from the Old Testament. The people of the Old Testament celebrated, as we know, a special Jubilee every fifty years. We read about these in the Books of Leviticus and Deuteronomy. The Jubilee was to be a time when debts would be cancelled, when property was to be restored to families, and slaves given their freedom. It was to be a time of hope, and therefore of joy.

The author of the Book of Deuteronomy laid great

stress on the duty to care for the poor. We should note this point carefully for it applies as much today as it did to the people of the Old Testament. The poor, the suffering, the marginalised, these will be our special concern both in the period of preparation for the millennium and, of course, afterwards. It is a Gospel precept to care for those in need. We read in the Book of Deuteronomy:

> Do not harden your hearts or close your hands against that poor brother of yours, but be open-handed with him and lend him enough for his needs ... Always be open-handed with anyone in your country who is in need and poor.
>
> (Deuteronomy 15:7–11)

The most important event we are celebrating in the year 2000 is the Incarnation. Christ is the one who liberates, who forgives, who reconciles, who gives hope. Christ Our Saviour is the special favour from God. Christ is the Jubilee. The year of favour is today and every day. Christ is always present for us and amongst us. He searches all our hearts, each one of us, to see if we will respond to his call: 'Repent and believe the Gospel' (Mark 1:15).

❦

The need to recapture a sense of mystery

Today's sophisticated minds find it hard to believe that God became man, that he died on the cross and then rose again from the dead. These truths and much else in our Christian faith are often ignored in our contemporary culture. We have grown out of religion. We are now adult. Are we? I wonder. Can we not be humble enough to acknowledge that there could be a reality which we could not discover for ourselves? We need to recapture a sense of mystery.

A mystery is a truth which lies beyond us. It can be entered into, explored, inhabited even; but it can never be exhausted or fathomed. Our age dislikes intensely the idea of mystery, because it directly exposes our limitations. The thought that there could be something or someone beyond human comprehension or imagining is of course exciting, but it is also belittling. It puts us in our place and that place is not at the centre. Science has played an important role here, at once dispelling apparent mysteries and solving problems, and continually pushing forward the boundaries of human knowledge. The truth is that the whole scientific process is itself an exploration of an ordered creation, but it is an inherently limited one.

❦

Revealed truths

We believe not because we understand and see clearly the truths of our faith, but because we have been taught them by him who can neither deceive or be deceived. These truths are revealed. We accept them and then spend a lifetime exploring them. Happily we have an authentic teacher in the Church who, with the special help of the Holy Spirit, can guide us so that we do not deviate from the truth. The teacher is known by a Latin name, the magisterium.

The question of truth is, I believe, sometimes evaded. There is an attitude which says, 'Who can tell what is true? The only reason for being spiritual, or going to Church, is if you find it helpful, if it makes you feel better.' But of course it matters crucially whether God in fact exists, and whether Jesus Christ is in fact his Son sent to redeem us. If it is not true, if the central claims of Christianity are false, then we are deluded, worshipping a chimera.

On the other hand, if the claims of Christianity are true, then this transforms everything. The key question is whether or not Christianity is true. It cannot be true and yet at the same time not matter. So we focus our attention on the foundation of our belief, and the revealed truth in which we put our trust.

❧

The message of the millennium

There is no need for us Christians to tell each other why we are going to celebrate. We admit, of course, that two thousand years since the birth of Christ may be no more than an approximation to the actual date, but that is of little consequence. The date is acknowledged to be 'anno domini'. It is the fact that God became man and dwelt amongst us which is the reason for our celebration. We recognise this to be the central moment of history. The year 2000 cannot just be a continuous New Year's party. Indeed, for non-Christians who do not accept Jesus Christ as God made man, the beginning of a new millennium should mark a new beginning for them too. We want the world to be a better place and, presumably, we would like to be better people. That must include, surely, the reawakening of that spiritual instinct which I believe to be in each person.

Our personal change of heart must have its impact on society today. We live in a world in which and to which we are called to proclaim the year of the Lord's favour. Faith in Jesus Christ today means that tomorrow must be different, for us and for society. The call of Jesus is universal and personal. We are called to make a new start. That is the message of the millennium.

'All eyes in the synagogue were fixed on him' – and ours must be as well.

The Truth of Christmas

❧

Each Christmas we celebrate the truth that God became man. If you deny that truth or try to explain it away, then you cannot call yourself a Christian. Jesus Christ, true God and true man, Jesus Christ, Second Person of the Holy Trinity, became man, the Word became flesh and dwelt amongst us. This is what we profess, not only with our lips but with mind and heart.

It is one thing to repeat the formula 'God became man', quite another to be so affected by that truth that our personal lives are changed. Make no mistake about it: we are talking about 'good news' – news that should change lives and eventually change the world. You have heard this good news in past years, or when you were young, but it may have ceased to make any impact on you. The news is not stale. It is we who are stale, and we become so if we do not reflect prayerfully enough, and often enough, on the truth that should never cease to amaze us – namely, that God became man. Yes, there is a God. Yes, he became man; yes, it is important, vitally so.

What is there in that for me? That is a very modern question, a self-regarding view from people who are absorbed in self. The real question is a different one. Christ is asking us a question. 'Will you receive me into your life? Behold I am knocking at your door,' he says. Will you let him in or keep him out?

We have, I am afraid, squeezed God out of our culture, and so, paradoxically, we have almost succeeded in removing Christ from Christmas. Can you imagine, keeping Christ out of Christmas? Do you doubt it? Look into our shop windows, study our media, ask the reason for any Christmas party. What are you celebrating? It is not my intent to empty Christmas of enjoyment. Far from it: I want us to rediscover the real reason for partying and enjoyment. I want to put Christ back into Christmas.

There is a further point. We must not leave Christ out of the millennium, the Holy Year. We are in danger of doing so, partly because we have become a secular society – by which I mean a society that does not need God, or does not care about him – partly because of the foolish notion that we may offend others who do not accept Christ as we do. Other faiths will respect us if we are true to ourselves. We must, as Christians, proclaim the truth. God became man. He dwelt amongst us. That is good news. So may the news take root in our minds and hearts, and like a good seed germinate, grow and bear good fruit.

The Need to Bring Christ back into Christmas

🦋

The people of God had long awaited their Messiah and his coming was to be a time of joy, of peace, of all things being made well. But they were shrewd enough to know that other forces would be at work, the ones that cause sadness instead of joy, war instead of peace. Indeed they knew by instinct and by the guidance of the Holy Spirit that the Messiah himself would be ill-treated and abused. It is that change from light to darkness and from darkness to light which is the rhythm of our twenty-four hours, and the rhythm of our history.

The prophets of the Old Testament reminded Israel time and again that God was with them, but in their political life the people of Israel were constantly in bondage, and their selfishness brought poverty and oppression to others, though they would in bad times turn to God to help them break from the shackles that held them.

Is it any different now? Strange, is it not, that the Messiah has come – and not just a national charismatic figure but God made man for us. Yet there is the same rhythm of light and darkness. We know that Christ has come and we renew our faith in that fact. We acknowledge him as the radiant light of God's glory. We acknowledge him as the Son appointed to be inherent in all things, and we bow down and adore the Word that was made flesh. We know too that there are many, past and present, who are truly Christian in their lives and outlook: those who strive for that fullness of life which he came to give.

But what of Christianity? Is ours a world that lives by the Gospel? Can we say there is true peace on earth? Can we stand up and affirm that there is no poverty in our world? Can we boast that every human being is treated with the respect which the dignity of humanity requires?

Christ has come. There are people who are Christians in behaviour and attitude, thank God. But Christianity has yet to be achieved. Ours is not a Christian world. Our country is not a Christian country.

> He was in the world that had its being through him, and the world did not know him ... But all those who believe he empowered to become children of God. (John 1:10–12)

Darkness, curiously enough, has its fascinations. Light can often be too dazzling. It is easier and more comfortable not to know. But those words of St John go on, nonetheless, ringing in my ears.

If our Jubilee celebration is to have the meaning it should have, then we shall go forward somewhat changed and transformed. The grace of God is there for us to receive, the power to become the children of God, the followers of Christ. It is within our power to say yes or to say no, or perhaps, more frighteningly, to be lukewarm and tepid.

As this century goes forward into the next the great problems of the world become more complex, and human dignity more undermined as a result. It is for us as followers of Christ to resolve, with his power, to live our own lives by the Gospel which he came to preach, and to show by our attitude and example that this indeed is the good news which God has given to us, that God IS, that he sent his Son because he loves us. Through our following of him 'all things will be well, all manner of things will be well'.

❧

The truth of the Incarnation

It is always sad to meet a person who does not know God. It is sad too to meet a person who does, yet fails to realise the depth, the breadth and the warmth of God's love. That is a great sadness in anyone's life.

Even fewer people know and accept that God became man. All down the ages men and women have shied away from acknowledging and accepting that truth. They have tried to distort it, tried to make out either that he was not fully God or that he was not fully man. Many people, some in our own day, have tried to explain the whole thing away. With learned arguments they have

[130]

attempted to prove that it is not true that God became man because, they would say, it is not possible. Many have run away from the implications of God becoming man, the demands it can make, the change in behaviour that it can entail, the inconvenience to which we may be put.

But the truth is unmistakable and clear. We believe in one Lord Jesus Christ, the only Son of God, eternally begotten of the Father. Yes, he is truly God, and truly man. The Church sings or recites this every Sunday of the year in order to impress it on our minds with its simplicity and its clarity, and that is what we celebrate in the year 2000, the Jubilee year.

Celebrating the Incarnation

❧

The role of Our Blessed Lady

In the year 2000 we shall be celebrating in a most solemn manner the birth of Our Lord. The Church lives through Advent again – waiting and preparing. Mary is present and as mother. She points to her Son, the Word that became flesh, to God who became man.

The birth of Mary constituted a new beginning for humanity. She was part of God's plan to put right the tragic result of sin in our own personal times and in our society as a whole. But sin never touched Mary for she was conceived immaculate. She was born perfect – full of grace and, surely, gifted with all those human qualities which we instinctively admire. She was understanding, compassionate, affectionate, with a presence that inspired confidence in others weaker and more fragile than she was. I believe that all who met her were immediately drawn to her. She had an attractive personality. People wanted to be with her.

She had been fashioned by God to be the perfect mother, for to be mother was and is her special role.

She was the mother of Jesus and now is the Mother of the Church. Indeed her birth heralded, as it were, the birth of Jesus and the birth of the Church.

The nativity scene is well imprinted on the minds of Christ's followers. The faithful have knelt often enough at the crib and adored the image of the Child before them, the God whom they know and acknowledge as a result of their faith.

That belief in the fact that the Word became flesh, that the Second Person of the Blessed Trinity became man, is the basis of our Christian faith. Affirming this truth is important, too, to appreciate fully Mary's role as Mother of the Church and the part she must play in our lives. The Church was born on Calvary; its mission began at Pentecost. Mary was present on both occasions, and always in her role as Mother.

Calvary was that special 'hour' about which her Son often spoke, the hour of his glorification through death and resurrection, and of our redemption and salvation from sin. You remember how he said to her, 'Mary, behold your Son' and to John, at that moment representing all humanity, 'Behold thy Mother'.

She points to him, the Word that became flesh, to God the Son who became man, and she says to us what she told the waiters at Cana: 'Do whatever he tells you' (John 2:5).

Faith in the Incarnation

❧

The eyes of faith

We are without the light and cannot see. There is nothing wrong with the light, but there is much wrong with our eyes. Our eyes are weak and incapable of seeing the light. They need to be healed first, and strengthened afterwards. I am speaking about the eyes of faith.

It is that power given to us by God himself which enables us to say 'I believe', the gift of faith given to us when we were baptised. We can extinguish that light, or we can ignore it – or we can try to see it more clearly.

As we make our act of faith in the Incarnation – the great mystery of God becoming man – we ask humbly, but insistently, that our sight be restored, the eyes of faith healed and strengthened so as to be able to say with strong conviction: Yes, I believe that God became man, and the Word was made flesh and dwelt amongst us; that he is my way, that he gives me truth, gives me life, the life that comes through the Sacraments, and comes in full measure when we receive him in Holy Communion.

❧

God became man

The words are simple and direct, but their meaning far beyond our power to comprehend. Our eyes do not see, our touch is of no avail. The agnostic in us struggles with the believer we wish to be. Often we only half believe. But it is not flesh and blood that leads us to the truth. It is our Father in heaven who gives us the light to say 'I do believe' and with conviction. His touch is gentle. There is no force as he moves us to share his secret thoughts. He, Emmanuel, is God amongst us, a man to lead us where we truly belong, wrapped in his love for us.

This is the time to make space in our heart for him to enter, to make his claim deep within. He comes to those who open wide the door. There must be room for him, the eternal and the infinite to be at one with us.

Would there be room for you and for me around that manger in the crib? Can we share a place among the angels and shepherds? The angels marvelled at the glory of God which they could see and that sight called forth from them that special song: 'Glory to God in the highest …'. The shepherds were the first among us to see the child, and on seeing him they discovered the truth of what had been told them about this child.

But the shepherds did not see what the angels saw. Nor do we share the vision which the angels know. We do not see God as he is, for no man can see him and live. The greatness of his majesty is too much for our frailty. We could not bear, or dare, to see him face to face until prepared and strengthened so to do. But in the presence of that small child we are at ease like the shepherds. We are not overwhelmed, and now we look at the child and see the truth of what has been told about him. We see one thing, a small child; we believe another, God made man.

We do not see what the angels saw but we believe what the shepherds understood, and we believe more clearly as our faith grows stronger. Faith, not vision, makes us sing the angels' song: 'Glory to God in the highest'. It is a song of blind people who have not seen, but have heard the good news and understood. There is a gentle peace in the singing of that song. It is the peace that comes from giving glory to God, of reaching beyond where thought and word can take us – into God's world.

The humble sing for they have generous hearts, hearts moved by God, hearts which have their reasons beyond the weakness of their minds.

Faith, a Star to Guide Us

❦

Faith is like a star. It is a gentle light, a lesser light from time to time obscured by clouds, and not always as bright as the traveller might wish. It is in no way as good as the sun, but it is enough each day to be able to see perhaps just one step ahead. Faith is a small light but a very important one.

Vision is like the sun. Nothing can hide from the midday sun, everything is revealed. So it will be when we shall see God face to face in vision. But now it is faith, and vision is something for the future and to which we already look forward with happy anticipation.

If you follow the star of Bethlehem you will find just a child in the manger, or so it might seem, but it is faith which enables us to know that this child is truly God as well as truly man; not that we can see it clearly. Faith is a lesser light, but enough, and it is a light given by God, a special gift, his most important gift to us.

So as we travel through life we have the star to guide us, and we look for God and the will of God in everyday things, in persons and events and in many things.

We might just have seen the child in the manger and missed the point – that he is also God. Equally, we can go through life meeting people, loving people, and also miss the point. We can see only with our physical eyes, so we have to let that little light which is faith lead us to God who is, in some wonderful manner, within all things. If we look for him every day in our present situation in this life then we will most certainly find him. All the time our eyes are being trained to see him in the full glare of vision. That is our ultimate expectation.

Our Lord's Teaching
in the Beatitudes

❦

The teaching of Our Lord, summed up in what are called the Beatitudes, may seem strange to those unfamiliar with them. For instance, we are told we are truly happy – or blessed – when we are persecuted for the sake of righteousness, when we are reviled or when all kinds of evil are uttered against us. This is strange indeed, yet what he was doing in his teaching was to introduce us into a world where values are different from those we ourselves instinctively embrace. Who wants to be persecuted? Who wants to be reviled? Who wants to have falsehoods uttered against them?

But there is more to the teaching of Jesus in the Beatitudes. He is instructing us about the kind of people we should be:

- We should be poor in spirit, that means being fundamentally humble, recognising our limitations,

knowing we are dependent on each other, and
ultimately on God.

- We should be meek, not the meekness born of weakness, but meekness born of strength.
- We should be gentle with people – always the skill of
a person in control of himself or herself.
- We should be pure of heart, and the 'heart' in the
Bible is the very centre of our inner selves, the place
where I am truly me, that centre into which few can
penetrate save only God. Being pure of heart means
that nothing sordid, nothing base, nothing evil
should be found there.

In that same teaching we are also exhorted to hunger
and thirst for righteousness, for all that is holy, all that
is right, all that is good. We are told to be merciful, to
be peacemakers, and to accept and mourn the losses
that will surely be ours.

What are we to make of all this, especially when we
are told to 'rejoice and be glad' when we are persecuted, when we are pure in spirit and pure in heart?
Why? 'For your reward will be great in heaven.' We
arrive now at the central point in the teaching of Jesus
in the Beatitudes, reminding us that we are made for
happiness – another word for that is 'beatitude'. But
true happiness will only be ours in a different context
from this world. It is called heaven, when we shall see
God as he is. That experience will be one of ecstatic joy
which will have no end, no limitation. We are in fact
made for that.

So that is the kind of people we should be: poor in

spirit, pure in heart, merciful, striving for holiness, peacemakers. He tells us not to fret, not to be depressed when we meet contradictions or problems, persecution even, or all manner of suffering. None of these must be desired for themselves, nor should we seek such adversity. But when we encounter them we should recognise their value which is to remind us that we have here no abiding city, and that true happiness is for later on, not now.

You may be wondering how relevant all this is to people with a living to be earned, homes to run, a community to be served. Is the language of the Beatitudes too strange and therefore with no meaning? Not so. That teaching of Our Lord is for everyone, not only because it is good in itself but because it tells us how human beings should function in order to be properly and fully human, and this is a vital point: those who live as the Lord taught in the Beatitudes discover deep down a happiness and peace of which they will not be deprived by any person or circumstance. You need proof of that? Then seek out a person – priest or lay – who has been in prison in Eastern Europe, say, for conscience sake and you will know what I mean; you meet people who are free, at peace, serene. You are in the presence of greatness.

What a wonderful society ours would be if we were to live as Jesus taught us, for in embracing his values we would inevitably establish a society that was truly just and respectful of all people, and where those two vital aspects of life were given every esteem and protection. What a dream, what a vision. But with a change of heart among all of us we could establish such a society where there would be true order, God's order, and tranquillity resulting from order is peace. Look at the world around us. Is there peace? And in our society, have we true peace, that good ordering of society? Peace is born in the heart of each one of us. It starts with each one of us, and that change of heart comes only if we become men and women of true prayer. That, I think, is probably for most of us the greatest contribution we can make for peace in the world.

Human Love

❧

I have often said that the soul of this generation will be won or lost over the basic moral issues of life and love. We have suffered serious setbacks because of parliamentary decisions on embryology and human fertilisation. Abortion legislation has been dangerously extended. Destructive experimentation on human embryos in the first 14 days of their existence is, I fear, but the beginning of even more drastic assaults on human dignity and the sanctity of life.

Human love and relationships have publicly become increasingly trivialised in an atmosphere of sexual permissiveness which almost denies the possibility of exclusive and life-long commitment. One of the problems is that we have divorced human love and sexuality. I think that the freedom which many people allow themselves to express their sexuality here and there as they want, must be corroding human relationships. Many are not prepared to acknowledge that love requires self-sacrifice and discipline. We have to rediscover the value of true love. True love is not just getting what we want because we desire it. It means self-sacrifice, thinking of other people first.

❧

The meaning of love

I cannot begin to emulate the lyrical character of the Song of Songs, that great hymn of praise to human love. Nor, of course, could I or anyone else discover the depth of meaning the Lord gives to that word 'love'. We read in the Book of Genesis how human love had its origin in God himself; how, too, he had written its promptings and demands into our human nature. It is not good for us to be alone, we read. We need another, or others, to satisfy the cravings of our human hearts. We need to love and be loved.

But there are different kinds of love: the love of friendship, and that of the parent; the loving of the single person and that of the celibate, and married love. Each has its own rules to be learned and observed, rules that protect the beauty of love as thorns protect the rose. Perhaps one of the urgent needs of our time is to deepen and purify our concept of love.

Human love is precious because it is the entry into another's secret domain – that is, into his or her inner self, where none may enter except the beloved.

Human love is rewarding for it brightens up the day and makes the burdens of life easier to carry. It is a gentle companion when pain or tragedy afflicts us.

Human love is a gift. Often we do not know whence it comes, until we begin to see that its origin is in one who is of all lovers the most loving. There is a moment of intuition when we see that God *is* and that God is love.

Our human love helps us, then, to explore the meaning of that word in him. But speaking about love is one thing, living it another. It makes demands. St Paul spells that out for us when he says that love is not jealous, boastful, conceited, rude, self-seeking, easily taking offence or harbouring grievances. It is patient, kind, feels no envy and claims no rights (1 Corinthians 13:3, 4).

That is not a bad checklist. We have to be able to dream dreams and strive after ideals. The promises you make are solemn ones. If you have any mental reservations then your gift of yourself to the other is neither true nor authentic. A provisional agreement, as it were, will inevitably come to grief and finish. A genuine one will lead to something very wholesome and beautiful.

❦

Friendship

There always comes a moment which you can never quite catch or define – you only know it has happened. It is a moment when an acquaintance becomes a friendship. In a sense it has been happening all the time, but sometimes you are aware of a particular moment. I suspect, too, that there is a moment when a friend becomes a lover. In a sense the change from one to the other has been taking place over a period of time, but there comes a point when we know that we can trust the other, exchange confidences, keep each other's secrets. We are friends.

This is paralleled in the spiritual life. Holiness involves friendship with God. The movement towards the realisation of God's love for us, and ours for him, is similar to our relationship with other people. There has to come that moment, a touch by the Holy Spirit turning that acquaintance with God into friendship. He ceases to be a Sunday acquaintance and becomes an everyday friend. It doesn't come suddenly, because you cannot have a friendship unless there is first acquaintance. Our part in making this happen is fidelity to prayer and the Sacraments.

※

Married love

The love that brings two people together is not strong enough to keep them together. That love must deepen, perhaps even change in the ups and downs of life, for love is an art to be learned, no doubt the achievement of a lifetime. In married love, when two people become one at every level of their being, and if God so decrees, they engage in that greatest of human achievements, the creation of new life and thus become co-workers, co-creators with God.

'My beloved is mine and I am his . . . Set me like a seal on your heart' (Song of Songs). Are those not words which God speaks to each one of us? He, too, wishes to be a seal on our hearts. When such a thought begins to prompt your prayers and your actions, you are then beginning to discover true religion. This applies to all of us, married or not.

St Paul, on more than one occasion, and notably when writing to the Corinthians, was quite uncompromising about the qualities which love must have. To the Philippians he wrote:

Always consider the other person to be better than yourself, so that nobody thinks of his own interests first, but everyone thinks of other people's interests instead. In your minds you must be the same as Christ Jesus. (Philippians 2:3–5)

True love is a precious gift from God. It reflects what God is: as St John wrote, God is love. True love among humans must be ever faithful and permanent. Fidelity and permanence belong to the very nature of the marriage bond.

❦

The family

The family is the first school of life and love. Each of us is marked indelibly by our own family and childhood experience. If the child sees in its parents not a perfect marriage (for what marriage can ever be that?) but one that is good enough, then that example will fashion the child's own attitude to marriage. If, on the other hand, this is not the child's experience, then not only will it be disillusioned with marriage, more profoundly perhaps the child will lose its sense of trust in the adult world.

Family life is, I know, very difficult today. Many people have less time together, more concerns about money and employment, greater stress. The stable family is constantly undermined in our culture. Fidelity and lifelong commitment are too often seen as hopelessly idealistic or even undesirable.

Our Lord celebrated children: '. . . do not keep them back from me; the Kingdom of Heaven belongs to such as these' (Matthew 19:14). He placed them first, and so should we. The calling to be a parent is an important vocation. Children learn to love because they have first been loved. It must be very hard for a child who has not experienced human love to believe that God loves them.

❧

High ideals

The Church's teaching presents humanity with very high ideals – about love, the sacredness of sexual relations, the exclusiveness and permanence of every marriage, and responsible parenthood. But in fact the Church is only pointing to what it is to be human, and therefore what it is that human beings need for their deepest well-being and fulfilment. The gap between the Church's understanding of marriage and some values and attitudes prevalent in our culture today is all too obvious. The idea of marriage as a permanent lifelong commitment, or of confining sexual relationships to one partner, are seen by many today as unattainable fantasies, far removed from reality.

In fact, I would argue the exact opposite. It strikes me that in our society's elevation of freedom of choice to the apparent exclusion of other values, and its seemingly endless obsession with sex manifested in so much of the media today, what we are witnessing is the peddling of unreal fantasies about what it is to be human, false promises of what makes for human happiness. The Church's teaching, in contrast, confronts us head on with the realities of responsible choice and the obligations which flow from making binding commitments to others.

The Church has both to preach and to live by the Gospel. That means we have to be clear about moral principles, and unafraid to state unpalatable truths, such as that fornication and adultery are wrong. At the same time, if we are to live the Gospel we must always be compassionate, and do all we can to help and support those in difficulty or distress.

❧

The potential of the millennium

We have a vision in Christ of what humanity is called to be and is struggling to become. We need to speak and act with confidence, to advocate and witness to the possibility of a human society being transformed by the renewing power of God's life and love; to hold hard to those values which alone can restore moral health and spiritual vitality. We can only do this by praying for the perseverance to keep walking on the journey of faith.

The millennium must become a moment of genuine renewal and new beginnings for our society. It is a sacred time, a Jubilee, and if the imaginations of enough people catch fire with enthusiasm, it has immense potential to inspire a spiritual renewal on both a personal and a national level.

Witness: as Followers of Christ

❧

The potter

You, Lord, are our Father; we the clay, you the potter. (Isaiah 64:8)

I once read something written in the year 300 AD; it said this: 'Whatever was the form and expression given to the clay by the Creator, Christ was in his thoughts as one day to become man.' When God fashioned you, when God made me, he was trying to create something from the model in his head. That model is Jesus Christ his Son. The more he could make us like Jesus Christ, the more would we be that perfect work which he wanted to have.

All through life he is trying to fashion us, shape us, model us, so that increasingly we become more like Jesus Christ, with the same values, the same reactions, the same way of doing and serving. Because surely if we always need, as we do, a standard to reach, there can be no standard other than Jesus Christ. So true is that, that I firmly believe you cannot be a full human being unless you become more and more like him.

What a standard that is. No, it does not mean just having virtues, it does not mean just being a nice person. It is a terrifying ideal, because it means too that sometimes we shall suffer as he suffered, be despised, be criticised, be written off, have everything said against us. When life is not going our way, we get annoyed. How often we forget that if we are going to be true followers of Jesus Christ, it will demand making sacrifices, facing problems and difficulties.

Today, perhaps more than any time in our history, the Christian witness is badly needed. If we the baptised Christians do not rise to the occasion, then we fail as Christians to shape society and mould it as God wishes it to be. 'Lord, you are our Father; we the clay, you the potter.' We can think and pray about that constantly. We are all the work of that potter's hand, who fashions the clay: God our Father, lovingly and with pride, fashioning us.

No potter sets about his task unless he loves what he is doing, and loves the work which he has done. So it is with God. He loves us and loves to work on us. Then he knows that through us the power of Christ can transform, not only us but the world in which we live. That, and no less than that, is the destiny of a Christian community.

The Evening of Life

❦

The respect due to the elderly

The years of the Second World War were a time of unparalleled national unity and idealism. There was a feeling that when we emerged from the struggle against Hitler, we would be ready to reshape society, to make our land a fairer, more decent place in which to live. We were standing up not just for national survival but for certain fundamental civilised values, for freedom and human dignity.

Sadly, not all our dreams came to pass. Some of the values we fought for have been challenged and rejected in the years since the war. The absolute sanctity and integrity of human life is being flagrantly violated. There is a spirit of violence, vandalism and lawlessness in our society that would have appeared alien to us half a century ago. Church-going has declined but there is a new spirit of Christian unity, and the hunger for the things of God persists.

Our society is strongly influenced by commercial and materialistic considerations. That may help to explain why we often fail to acknowledge the debt society still owes in justice to its older members who may not now be so commercially significant, but in the past have contributed greatly to our present prosperity. It does not, though, explain why we so often undervalue the talent and energy of older people which represents an untapped resource our society clearly needs. Those in their 'third age' can bring valuable experience and expertise to many tasks. Above all they can contribute a quality so often absent from our conduct of affairs. The hard-won wisdom of the old is an invaluable asset we squander to our cost. In the past societies have profited greatly from that wisdom and have revered their older members.

Society undoubtedly is both distorted and impoverished if it loses its sense of individual worth, if it fails to protect and cherish both its very young and its ageing members. Those who have now entered the so-called third age have already given much to their families and society. It is surely a matter of considerable concern that some elderly are now the new poor, left to struggle for mere survival.

Ultimately we all have to come to accept the decline of physical powers, and can no longer ignore the obvious fact that each life is a finite source. Some people have to endure long, painful, even humiliating illnesses. All of us in some way are called to share the cross of Christ. Here the Church and religious faith come into their own, offering meaning, hope and vision. Life is a gift from our Creator and we do not have absolute dominion over it. Nor do we have dominion over death; the timing of it is not of our choice, nor the manner of our dying. We accept death from the hand of God.

❧

Death, the final embrace

A materialist regards the end of human life as a decline into oblivion, the final chapter in each life the utter dissolution. The Christian believer, however, sees the final stage of life in terms of ascent towards the summit of human experience. Far from being the end, death is transition to new life, a necessary preliminary to eventual resurrection and unending life with God.

> In the eyes of the unwise, they did appear to die, their going looked like a disaster, their leaving us like annihilation, but they are in peace. (Wisdom 3:2–3)

Death is the final embrace of utter ecstasy when all that was good and wholesome among life's experiences will finally be given immortal significance.

Of course it is natural to be fearful of death, but it is over the years we begin to discover that love which God has for each of us – a love that is close, warm, intimate; then love does indeed cast out fear and death becomes no longer an awkward stranger I would rather not meet, but a friend I am happy to embrace. A religious vision influences profoundly and practically the process of ageing.

[154]

Age gives us time for reflection, for discernment. As we approach our final encounter with God, we should be witnesses to the enduring values in life. Life is a journey to God. As we walk we strive to love God and our fellow men and women. For me personally, the most profound truth of my faith is that there is Someone who loves me completely and totally in spite of my weaknesses and failures. That keeps me going.

※

Death, the gateway to the moment of ecstasy

From experience of contact with people from different walks of life, I have seen bewilderment before the problems that face our society today. I have detected that many are still haunted by such perennial problems as pain, suffering and death. This unease has been well expressed by a contemporary writer:

> Although man is reaching out towards the stars, he still feels anguish in his heart; although he has succeeded in transplanting vital organs such as the heart and kidney, he still trembles at the thought of death; although he has pleasure and comfort at his beck and call, he still has not succeeded in filling the bitter emptiness he feels within him. Although he has crowded into huge cities, he still feels a piercing loneliness. (Julian Arias, *The God I don't believe in*, Abbey Press)

Anguish in the heart, fear of dying. I want to know

what death means, and why life which I love and to which I want to cling, cannot go on for ever. The basic questions are: What is the meaning of death? What is the purpose of life?

There is in humanity's situation an in-built contradiction. We are creatures of desire, looking always for that which gives total and permanent satisfaction, craving all the time that which will finally meet our noblest and best aspirations. On the other hand, the object or the person which can give us this satisfaction eludes us. Are we destined then to be forever unfulfilled? If this world is all, then it looks as if we have to settle for being unsatisfied, frustrated. It is this dilemma which prompts the human mind to try to resolve the contradiction. It is one of those experiences that should set us on the way to search for God.

In what experience does human happiness reach its highest point? I suggest that it is in the experience of love. Strip that word of all that debases or degrades it, and love stands as man's greatest – and indeed most difficult – achievement. It is the scene of his happiest successes and of his saddest failures. A strong loving relationship between two persons is what comes closest to giving that complete and unending happiness. But not quite, for there is always the threat of impermanence. In any case, can another person meet totally all our natural and instinctive longing to have all our cravings and desires satisfied? I do not think so. Only that which is totally lovable from every point of view is in the end adequate. We want to be united with that most lovable of all, totally and for ever. It is for that union that we were made. That makes sense of death, for death is then seen as the natural event which puts us on the way to that moment of ecstasy – to behold that which is most lovable, and thus to be locked in that unending embrace which we call union with God.

I think it is very natural for all of us to have a certain fear of death. A lot of people will express it by saying that they are frightened of dying but not frightened of being dead. I think the idea of dying makes people very vulnerable. Also there is a very common temptation to question whether there is really anything after death. That temptation can come back even after we have experienced a kind of certitude that all is well. I think it often returns to people as they are dying and can be a very considerable trial to them, a very dark tunnel they go through. I have to answer by saying that the human mind is a very limited thing: we cannot see beyond this present life.

There is deep within each one of us, normally, the desire to live. We want to hang on to life, we don't want to leave our friends. However difficult life may have been, we want to hold on to it. That is a very deep instinct and it is my firm belief that through prayer, through reading, through reflection, faith teaches us that there *is* something beyond death, that life is not absurd, that it is not going to end in frustration. It is faith in the person of Jesus Christ, God who became man, who died and rose again from the dead. *That* is the key. When you have got that firmly in your mind and heart, then you can say: 'Into your hands, Lord, I commend my spirit.' That prayer, which I pray almost daily, is the prayer of Our Lord himself when he was dying on the cross.

I say that prayer very often because it is a prayer of complete trust in God: 'I cannot solve this, Lord, but into thy hands I commend my spirit.' To me, the fact that the Son of God, dying on the cross, prayed that prayer gives it a very special significance.